OPERATION
NEPTUNE

OPERATION NEPTUNE

The Inside Story
of Naval Operations for
the Normandy Landings 1944

by

Vice-Admiral B. B. Schofield,
CB CBE

Pen & Sword
MILITARY

First published in 1974 by Ian Allen Ltd
Published in this format in Great Britain in 2008 by
Pen & Sword Military
an imprint of
Pen & Sword Books Ltd
47 Church Street
Barnsley
South Yorkshire
S70 2AS

ISBN 978 1 84415 662 7

A CIP catalogue record for this book is
available from the British Library

Typeset in Sabon by
Phoenix Typesetting, Auldgirth, Dumfriesshire

Printed and bound in England by
Biddles Ltd, King's Lynn

Pen & Sword Books Ltd incorporates the Imprints of Pen & Sword
Aviation, Pen & Sword Maritime, Pen & Sword Military, Wharncliffe
Local History, Pen & Sword Select, Pen & Sword Military Classics and
Leo Cooper.

For a complete list of Pen & Sword titles please contact
PEN & SWORD BOOKS LIMITED
47 Church Street, Barnsley, South Yorkshire, S70 2AS, England
E-mail: enquiries@pen-and-sword.co.uk
Website: www.pen-and-sword.co.uk

Contents

'Tis not in mortals to command success
But we'll do more, Sempronius: we'll deserve it

Addison

Introduction

The employment of ships to move armies to positions of strategic advantage from which they could attack the enemy more effectively is one of the recurrent themes in the history of warfare. It was exploited successfully by the Greeks and Romans and some later examples of its use are seen in Drake's campaign in the West Indies in 1585, Philip II of Spain with his famous Armada in 1588, and the Swedish warrior King Gustavus II Adolphus between 1628 and 1632. In the Seven Years War (1756–63) Britain used this principle, notably with the capture of Quebec in 1759 and also in the American War of Independence (1775–78), with unhappy results, as well as in alliance with France during the Crimean War (1853–56).

It is all the more surprising, therefore, that these historical precedents should have had almost no influence on military thought when, in the early part of this century, the possibility of war between Britain and Germany, with France as an ally of the former, came to be considered. The British Admiralty and War Office held conflicting views as to how to make the best use of the country's military (using the term in its widest sense) power. Admiral Sir John (Jacky) Fisher, First Sea Lord from 1906 to 1910, dominated Whitehall during those crucial years. He regarded the Army as a projectile to be fired by the Navy in accordance with plans which it was the prerogative of the Senior Service to formulate and keep very much to itself! There was at the time much discussion about the threat of a German invasion and how many troops would be needed to repel it. Fisher's attitude was characteristic: "To assign to the Army co-responsibility with the Navy for the defence of the United Kingdom was to misconceive the fundamental principle of the problem."[1] In the event the War Office went ahead with its own plans for the unopposed landing of an Expeditionary Force in France to support the left flank of the French Army. When war broke out in 1914, Fisher had been four years out of office and the Navy had no option but to go along with the War Office plan. By the time Fisher was reinstated it was a *fait accompli.* Then in 1915 Churchill persuaded the Government to authorise a great amphibious operation to capture the Gallipoli peninsula from the Turks and open the way to Constantinople, although no specialised equipment, such as amphibious operations demand, was available. "An amphibious assault is one of the most difficult of military operations," writes David Syrett. "Detailed planning and considerable skill are required to transfer an army from ship to shore in battle formation,"[2] and he goes on to recall how, in 18th century operations, it had been found that special flat-bottomed boats were essential and that, in 1776 at Staten Island, the army built a number of craft capable of carrying 100 soldiers and having ramps mounted in their bows for unloading cannon.

After the failure of the Gallipoli campaign no further attempts were made during World War I to exploit the use of sea power by carrying out amphibious operations, although a landing on the Belgian coast, with the object of turning the enemy's flank and recapturing the Belgian ports, was proposed by the Navy but rejected by the Army.

In the twenty years between World Wars I and II amphibious operations involving the Navy, Army and newly fledged Air Force were given little consideration. The experience of the Dardanelles was graven deep into the minds of senior officers. At the Staff Colleges, however, paper exercises involving all three services were carried out and a Manual of Combined Operations was compiled, but it was little more than an outline of the problems involved. Still, some good came out of these paper battles, since it brought the officers of the three services together and enabled then to gain an insight into each other's problems. During the author's time at the Naval Staff College in 1934 the subject chosen for study, ironically enough, was the recapture of Singapore from the

Japanese! Two years later, in 1936, a far-seeing Director of the College, Captain (later Vice-Admiral) B.C. Watson submitted a paper to the Board of Admiralty based on the results of the studies referred to above, made by three Service Staff Colleges. In it he warned that, unless some practical steps were taken, the Services would find themselves ill-prepared to carry out Combined Operations such as a future war might demand. He went on to recommend the setting up of an Interservice Committee and a training and development centre to study the whole problem and to develop the appropriate specialised material; also that the role of naval ships for bombardment should be considered, and the way in which aircraft could best be used. It was not, however, until two more years had elapsed and the Deputy Chief of the General Staff, General Sir Ronald Adam, put in an equally well reasoned plea for action, that the Chiefs of Staff gave the proposals their blessing and the Inter-Services Training and Development Centre (ISTDC) came into being. It was given a number of specific problems to examine, which included the design of ships suitable for landing tanks, the kind of beach organisation that would be required, as well as headquarters ships, floating piers, the design of amphibious tanks and beach obstacles, and how amphibious raids should be carried out. Little did the handful of specially selected officers who formed the staff of the organisation realise how vitally important the results of all their experiments were to prove in the not too distant future. One of its members, Captain (later Rear-Admiral) L.E.H Maund RN, had witnessed the Japanese landing at Shanghai and had noted the use made of specially constructed ships which were able to disgorge a large number of landing craft full of troops. One of the first proposals therefore, put forward by the ISTDC, was for a number of such ships to be constructed. They must be capable of high speed so that they could approach the enemy's coast during the darkness and discharge their landing craft, which would then approach the shore under cover of smoke and covered by gun support from destroyers, to seize a beach-head. Another force would then be landed to pass through the first one and capture positions far enough inland to secure the beach-head and the anchorage. Finally, transport vehicles and stores would be landed direct on to the beach from specially designed craft. This doctrine was accepted in principle and the next step was to design and build prototype vessels. For the larger landing craft carriers, four 18 knot cargo liners under construction for the firm of Messrs. Alfred Holt and Sons for their Far East trade, were designed with the help of the well-known shipbuilding firm of Messrs. Thornycroft. It was obvious that to effect a landing on a hostile shore in any strength, a large number of vessels and landing craft would be required, but apart from building a few prototypes and some 20 ton water-jet propelled Motor Landing Craft, it did not at the time appear necessary to start quantity production.

When war broke out in September 1939, the construction of a few landing craft had been authorised, but strange to say the ISTDC was closed down, to be reopened however at the end of the year. In the United States things were not much better. The Marine Corps, which had been founded in 1933, issued a Landing Operations Manual a year later. By 1938 the doctrine it propounded had been tested and adopted, but apart from a shallow draft, self-propelled craft known as Eureka, no types of Landing Craft had been designed. After an exercise off Puerto Rico in February 1941, in which specially equipped transports were used, a set of amphibious instructions was prepared for the use of the Army.

During the disastrous Anglo-French campaign in Norway in 1940, the few landing craft available proved their worth. Soon afterwards they joined the heterogeneous flotilla of gallant little ships which carried out the Dunkirk evacuation which, although a defeat was, as Chester Wilmot has written, "Britain's salvation. It rescued her from another disastrous war of attrition on the Western Front and released her strategy from the shackles of subordination to the land-bound doctrines of the French."[3]

Early in the war, when the future trend of operations was still undecided, the Admiralty requisitioned fifty large and valuable passenger ships for conversion to armed merchant cruisers. It was not until five of them had been lost, of which two, the *Rawalpindi* and the *Jervis Bay*, in circumstances which earned them undying renown, that it became apparent that these ships would be better employed as troop transports for which, when fighting began in the Middle East, there arose a pressing demand. This was followed by the need to reinforce Singapore, and after that fortress fell to the Japanese and the United States entered the war and began to gather strength, the problem arose of ferrying that country's growing armies to the battlefields first of North Africa and later of Europe, for which United States shipping was inadequate. Without the two giant passenger ships *Queen Mary* and *Queen Elizabeth*, generally referred to as the 'Monsters', this could not have been accomplished. From the outbreak of war to December 1945 these two ships, between them, carried 4,400,000 passengers of which the majority were troops, the number carried on each voyage being gradually increased until, in the months preceding the Normandy invasion, it reached the staggering figure of 15,000 on the west to east transatlantic voyages.

However, troops need equipment and this too had to be transported across the oceans to where it was needed. The ordinary four-hold cargo ship is far from ideal for the transport of such awkward loads as tanks, guns and trucks, which the highly mechanised armies of today demand in ever-increasing numbers. But these were the only ships available in any quantity so they had to be used, and, as will be seen later, they were constantly in short supply. Moreover, their use had to be balanced against that needed to maintain the British war effort, which necessitated importing enough raw materials to keep the factories supplied, and enough food to keep the population from starving since, unlike the United States, Britain only produced enough to feed about half her people. A shipping problem of a different character but equally important was the import of petroleum products to keep the Royal Air Force flying, the Fleet at sea, and to enable the Army to train for the battles which lay ahead, as well as to keep a proportion of the wheels of industry turning.

As the fighting in the Middle East grew in intensity, the demands of the armies there increased, and the Mediterranean being closed to shipping from the time Italy entered the war in 1940, supplies to that theatre had to be sent round the Cape of Good Hope, a voyage roughly four times as long. This greatly reduced the capacity of the shipping employed in keeping these armies supplied so that when, after the defeat of the Axis forces in North Africa, it was found possible to reopen the Mediterranean, it was estimated that this was equivalent to an increase in shipping availability of one million tons.

Due to the differences in the manner of operating shipping as between Britain and the United States, there was at first considerable difficulty in making a forward assessment of shipping availability, which in any case was dependant on the progress made in defeating the U-boats in the Battle of the Atlantic. However, the size of the forces which could be transported was dependent on the tonnage available, and without an estimate of this, the military planners could not make progress. The author had personal experience of this when, as Director of the Trade Division of the Admiralty in April 1943, he accompanied a small delegation, comprising representatives of the War Office, Ministry of War Transport, and Sea Transport to Washington D.C., to examine with our American opposite numbers, the feasibility from a shipping point of view of launching a cross Channel operation. It was by no means a simple issue as, in addition to the factors mentioned above, there was a difference of opinion between the British and American representatives regarding the figure to be used in calculating the number of tons per man by which stores and equipment, and therefore shipping space needed, are determined. As I have recounted elsewhere,[4] the issue was finally resolved at the eleventh hour, and it was estimated that the 3½ million deadweight tons of shipping which we found was needed to supply the great army which it was planned to land in France the following year, could be made available. This figure, however, did not include the very large number of landing ships and landing craft of various kinds which would be needed for the assault and follow up. These play a large part in the story of Operation Neptune, so brief descriptions of the principal types and the short titles by which they became known are given below. Further details are shown in Appendix I.

Landing Ship Infantry (LSI) These were ocean-going passenger ships or cargo liners equipped to transport troops to the area of the assault. They were equipped to carry a number of landing craft at davits into which the troops were transferred on reaching their destination. They were subdivided into three categories according to their size, Large, Medium, and Small indicated by the letters (L), (M) and (S) and the troop capacity varied from 1,500 to 200.

Landing Ship Tank (LST) A specially designed ship of about 3,000 tons displacement, capable of carrying 500 tons of tanks, vehicles and stores which were discharged over a ramp in the bows. They had a speed of about 12 knots and were armed with two 4in (10cm) smoke mortars, four 2pdr (pounder) and six 20mm A/A guns and had a complement of 98. Typical loads were eighteen 30-ton tanks, or thirty three-ton trucks and 217 troops.

Landing Craft Tank (LCT) A smaller version of the LST, displacing about 300 tons with a speed of 10 ½ knots and armed with two 2pdr or two 20mm A/A guns. A typical load was three 40-ton tanks. As the war progressed larger types were built.

Landing Craft Assault (LCA) A lightly armoured craft displacing ten tons with a crew of four and a speed of 6 knots armed with one machine gun. They could be hoisted at standard davits and had a capacity of 35 troops or 800lb (363kg) of stores. Their loaded draught was 18 inches (46cm).

Landing Craft Mechanised (LCM) The early types displaced 36 tons loaded, later ones 115 tons. Powered by petrol or diesel engines driving twin screws to give a speed of 7 ½ to 11 knots. They had bullet-proof bulwarks and steering position. They were designed primarily to carry one tank and some were capable of being hoisted with the load onboard.

As soon as he took office as Chief of Combined Operations in 1941, Admiral Lord Louis (later Earl) Mountbatten foresaw that there would be a great demand for ships of the above types which British production was unlikely to be able to meet. With the approval of the Chiefs of Staff, he therefore placed an order in the United States for 1,300 landing craft, stepped up soon after to 2,250. At the time the order was placed, there was some reluctance on the part of the Americans to accept it, but this attitude changed very quickly when they found themselves at war with Germany and Japan. In view of Britain's limited shipbuilding capacity compared with that of the United States, it was agreed that the former should concentrate mainly on the construction of landing craft and the latter on ships as well as craft.[5] As will be seen, a difference in procedure between the two countries over the allocation of landing ships and craft produced considerable difficulties in planning. The United States Navy, in particular, exercised strict control over its resources and resisted any interference in their allocation, even by the US Joint Chiefs of Staff.

As experience was gained with the amphibious landings in North Africa, Sicily, Italy and the Pacific, a great many variants of Landing Craft were produced. One of the most effective was the *Landing Craft Tank, Rocket (LCT (R))* mounting 800 to 1,000 5in rockets discharged simultaneously at a range of 3,000 yards (2,743m), the effect of which on the defending personnel was devastating, as survivors have testified.

In April 1942, as a result of a request by Admiral Mountbatten for a craft capable of crossing the Channel at a good speed and of carrying 200 men, the *Landing Craft Infantry (Large) (LCI (L))* was produced in the United States. Delivery of the first batch was effected in December 1942 and, after two years operating in the Mediterranean, they returned to the United Kingdom to take part in Operation Neptune.

The ingenuity displayed in the design and adaptation of Landing Ships and Craft, as well as in the production of special equipment, were some of the most important factors in the success of the Allied amphibious operations undertaken during World War II, which culminated in the invasion of Normandy. This fact was recognised when, after visiting the Assault area four days after the landing, the Chief of Staff of the United States Army, General Marshall, drafted a message to Admiral King, Field Marshal Sir Alan Brooke, General Arnold, Field Marshal Smuts and himself and which read:

10th June, '44

"Today we visited the British and American armies on the soil of France. We sailed through vast fleets of ships, with landing craft of many types pouring more and more men, vehicles and stores ashore . . . We wish to tell you at this moment in your arduous campaign (he was then Supreme Allied Commander, South East Asia) that we realise that much of this remarkable technique, and therefore the success of the venture has its origin in developments effected by you and your staff of Combined Operations."[6]

Notes

1 Professor Arthur Marder (ed.), *Years of Power*.
2 "The Methodology of British Amphibious Operations during the Seven Years and American Wars", *The Mariners Mirror*, August 1972.
3 Chester Wilmot, *The Struggle for Europe*.
4 B.B. Schofield, *British Sea Power*.
5 John Ehrman, *Grand Strategy*, Vol V.
6 Churchill, *The Second World War*, Vol VI.

Chapter One

Festung Europa

At the end of June 1940, the victory on land achieved by his armies found Hitler elated but with no clear idea as to what his next move should be. Britain was now his only active opponent but her situation was perilous. Although the bulk of the British Army had got away from Dunkirk, it had lost almost all its equipment and the Führer waited in hopeful expectation that Britain would come to terms. When, however, the peace offer which he made in the Reichstag on July 19, 1940 was firmly rejected, he ordered preparations to be made for an invasion of England, code-named Seelöwe (Sealion). The failure of the Luftwaffe to drive the Royal Air Force out of the sky during the Battle of Britain provided Hitler with a convenient excuse for suspending the invasion, an action which received the full support of the Heads of the German Army and Navy. It was known that he was reluctant to destroy Britain and the British Empire which he regarded as having a stabilising influence in the world. Nevertheless, even without invading England, had he concentrated Germany's war effort in an endeavour to defeat Britain by U-boat and air attacks, he might well have succeeded in bringing about her gradual starvation and ultimate collapse. In the event, his suspicions of Russia's intentions, his hatred of communism, and the threat which the Russian Army poised on his eastern frontier appeared to present, persuaded him that in order to make his rear secure, he must attack and defeat the Red Army. He argued that if he were to knock away Russia, one of the props on which he felt Britain might be relying, the other, the United States, would wither away and Britain would then be bound to sue for peace. This view was shared by Colonel General Halder, Chief of the General Staff, who wrote in his diary on July 31, 1940, "With Russia smashed, Britain's last hope would be shattered."[1]

The Commander in Chief of the German Navy, Grand Admiral Erich Raeder, who had little enthusiasm for Operation Seelöwe, did not favour an attack on Russia either. He pleaded for greater attention to be given to the Mediterranean which, he told Hitler, "the British have always considered the pivot of their world empire."[2] He suggested the seizure of Gibraltar and the Canary Islands, with the acquiescence of Spain, and assistance to Italy to achieve the capture of the Suez Canal and subsequently Palestine and Syria, circumstances which would oblige Turkey to adopt an Axis-orientated policy. "If we reach that point," he said, "Turkey will be in our power and the Russian problem will appear in a different light."[3] Although forced to admit the logic of Raeder's arguments, Hitler had come to regard the defeat of Russia both as an economic necessity and an essential step to safeguard himself against the possibility of being obliged to fight on two fronts. When, in September, a military alliance was successfully concluded between Germany, Italy and Japan, he used it as a means to silence his critics, pointing out that the resulting pressure on Russia and the United States, and British anxieties about her Far Eastern possessions would favour his design. In the event, the Japanese hedged their bet by signing a treaty of neutrality with Russia, then the successful British attack on the Italian fleet in Taranto and the defeat of Marshal Graziani's army in Libya by British forces under General Wavell early in 1941, obliged Hitler to come to the aid of his Axis partner Mussolini, first in North Africa and subsequently in Greece. This last named misadventure on the part of the Italian dictator obliged a postponement of the launching of the attack on Russia, known as Operation Barbarossa, and the loss of four weeks' good campaigning weather, a circumstance which was to be bitterly regretted by the German General Staff later in the year. Although the bulk of the German Army was committed to the attack on Russia, Hitler was compelled to retain some fifty divisions in the occupied countries of Norway, Denmark, Holland, Belgium and France to ensure their continued subjection. It was not, however, until things started to go wrong with the Russian offensive that he began to grow anxious about the situation in the West. In February 1942 he issued Directive Number 40, in which he laid down the basic organisation of command between the three services in the event of an Allied invasion in the West. Subsequently he issued a number of supplementary orders concerning the construction and strengthening of the defences in Western Europe, but in fact most of these were never implemented and he never visited the area to see for himself the true state of affairs. Directive Number 40 also endeavoured to settle the problem of inter-service relationships but since each service placed a different interpretation on it the result was increased friction between them. This became most noticeable over the question of the coast defences. Admiral Dönitz says, "Command of the coastal defences as a whole in the occupied countries was vested in the Army,"[4] and he goes on to explain that while for discipline, training, equipment and rations they were under the Navy, for operational purposes they were under the Army commander of the area concerned. But Order Number 40 laid down that they were under naval control so long as the enemy was afloat, but became an Army responsibility once a landing was effected, and post-war enquiries indicate that this was so.

Early in 1942 Hitler appointed the sixty-nine year old Field Marshal von Rundstedt, an extremely able if somewhat conservative general, to command the Western theatre. Known as the Field Marshal who had never lost a battle, he had retired at his own request in November 1941, having fallen out with the Führer over plans for a winter campaign in Russia. Von Rundstedt fully appreciated that, in accepting the position, he was sacrificing his principles for the sake of power. The task with which he was confronted was a formidable one. "I had over 3,000 miles of coast-line to cover," he told Sir Basil Liddell Hart when he interviewed him after the war, "from the Italian frontier in the south to the German frontier in the north and only 60 divisions with which to defend it. Most of them were low grade and some of them were skeletons."[5] Until 1943 France was used as a rest and regrouping area for German divisions mauled and exhausted from the fighting on the Russian front, and as a result there was a continual *va et vient* of troops which militated against the establishment of an efficient system of defence to meet the threat of invasion. Von

Rundstedt's first task, therefore, was to man the coast defences with permanent garrisons in each of the different sectors and to establish a number of strong points covering the ports. He then set about establishing mobile reserves at strategic points in the rear so that they could be moved up to reinforce a threatened area.

The Anglo-Canadian raid on Dieppe on August 19, 1942, shook Hitler to the extent that he ordered two of his best armoured divisions to be transferred from the Russian front to reinforce von Rundstedt's forces in the West. In the event only one of them arrived, the other having become engaged with the enemy before it could withdraw. German propaganda gave much prominence to the construction of an impregnable Atlantic Wall from Calais to the Spanish frontier, but it never existed west of Boulogne except as a figment of Goebbels' imagination. According to General Speidel, who became Chief of Staff to Army Group B in April 1944, "The whole development of coastal defence, that is to say the design and layout of the fortifications, had been entrusted to an engineer of the Todt organisation who was neither tactically nor strategically proficient, had no knowledge of the general war situation and no experience of co-operation with the armed forces."[6] Whatever the basic reason, lack of agreement between the Army, the Navy and the Todt organisation undoubtedly contributed to the slow progress made with the building of the Atlantic Wall, though the shortage of materials played its part. By the spring of 1944, except in the Pas de Calais, it consisted only of a series of strong points sited many miles apart along a 600 mile stretch of coast. They comprised radar installations, command posts and gun batteries, and the positions chosen were those covering places at which the German High Command suspected the Allies might attempt to land. They included Cap Gris Nez, the mouth of the Seine, the northern shoulder of the Cotentin Peninsula, the Channel Islands and the ports of Brest and Lorient. The Normandy coast between the Vire and the Orne was regarded by the German Navy as unsuitable for landing on account of its rocky outcrop and contained only a few field fortifications. However, before the Allied landing took place, a battery of 6in (15cm) guns was erected at Longues near Bayeux and another of 8in (21cm) guns at Marcouf on the east coast of the Cotentin Peninsula, both of which, as will be seen, were a considerable nuisance to the Allies.

The German Naval Command structure in France under Commander-in-Chief Naval Group West, Admiral Krancke, in Paris, comprised an Admiral commanding the Channel coast, with his headquarters at Rouen and under him were three subordinate commanders, viz. (i) the Pas de Calais command extending from the Belgian frontier south to the Somme; (ii) the Seine-Somme command covering the coast between those two rivers; (iii) the Normandy command from the Seine westwards to St. Malo. There was also an Admiral commanding the Atlantic coast with his head-quarters at Angers, who had three subordinate commanders, viz. Brittany, Loire and Gascony.

The limits of the naval commands did not coincide with those of the army, nor was there any close relationship between the naval, military and air authorities, which was essential if quick action were to be taken to meet rapidly changing circumstances such as might result from an Allied landing. The idea of a unified direction of command which Hitler envisaged was never realised.

In November 1943, Hitler appointed Field Marshal Erwin Rommel, one of Germany's most able Generals and former commander of the Afrika Korps, to inspect and improve the coast defences from Denmark down to the Spanish frontier. In Führer directive Number 51, dated November 3, 1943, he issued detailed instructions to all three services for a strengthening of the defences in the West. "I can no longer be responsible therefore, that the West should be further weakened in favour of another theatre of war," he said, and he ended the preamble with a warning to the Air Force and the Navy that they must expect heavy fighting in the air and on the sea and "engage in bold operations with all available ships." His instructions to the Navy included the following: "The Navy is to prepare the appropriate naval forces for the most difficult operation of the engagement of the enemy landing fleets. The development and readiness of existing coast defence craft is to be accelerated; the formation of additional coast batteries as well as the possibility of flank blockade to be explored." He went on to order the Navy to take similar steps for the defence of Norway and Denmark, the latter being given particular consideration. He concluded his directive, "I expect that in the time still remaining, all headquarters will make the greatest exertions to prepare for the expected decisive battle in the West.".[7]

Rommel's appointment as Inspector General of Coast Defences created some difficulty for von Rundstedt, but it was resolved when, at his own request, he was made Commander of Army Group B on January 15, 1944. This placed him directly under von Rundstedt's command. Rommel's experience in North Africa and in Italy had given him a healthy respect for the growing Allied Air power and he was convinced that von Rundstedt might find his reserves pinned down and unable to move when required to support a threatened area. He had also been deeply impressed by the quantity and variety of the landing equipment possessed by the Allies; he did not attach the same importance as his chief to their need to capture a port quickly in order to build up their strength and believed that for a time they could manage quite well without one. His naval adviser Vice-Admiral Friedrich Ruge, later to command the West German Bundesmarine, has written of him, "He was convinced that the campaign, indeed the whole war, would be lost if the invader were not thrown back into the sea within three days of landing."[8]

Rommel had a fertile mind and soon had his troops busy constructing all kinds of defences aimed at preventing a landing by Allied sea and air-borne forces. They included underwater obstacles made of wooden and iron piles driven into the sand below high water mark, to which explosives and booby traps were attached, jagged looking hedgehog obstructions, concrete dragon's teeth and lines of both moored and ground mines. Above high water mark the shore was to be mined in depth with land mines; flat areas suitable for the landing of gliders and parachute troops were to be obstructed with tree trunks and poles driven into the ground which became known as 'Rommel's asparagus'. He ordered the erection of coastal batteries and anti-tank guns in concrete emplacements thick enough to withstand bombing attacks, pill boxes containing machine guns to enfilade likely approaches, flame throwers, barbed wire and anti-tank ditches. Low lying areas were to be flooded and any gaps between them mined. While all men in forward units would be entrenched in fire-positions near the beaches, he wanted the armoured divisions with their tanks and guns stationed close behind the coast to prevent the inland penetration of enemy forces. Fortunately for the Allies, this ambitious programme was never completed. The effect of Allied bombing in Germany led to a withdrawal of labour to carry out urgent repairs in the homeland and there was considerable opposition from the commander of the armoured forces of Panzer Group West, General Geyr von Schweppenburg, to the positioning of his forces as suggested by Rommel. The matter was referred to Hitler who ordered a compromise solution which satisfied neither of the disputants and was militarily unsound, for he divided the control of the armoured forces between them so that neither a strong tactical nor strategic reserve could be created.

It would be an oversimplification of the difference of opinion between von Rundstedt and Rommel, regarding the steps to be taken to oppose an Allied landing, to say that the former favoured a defence in depth and the latter did not. Rommel wanted his defences to have depth but he wanted them to start at high water mark and extend inland five or more miles, whereas von Rundstedt envisaged the decisive battle taking place inland after the Allies had landed and before they had had time to build up their strength.

On March 20, 1944, Hitler discussed with the heads of his three Services and the commanders of the fortified regions of France, the question of an Allied landing. "It goes without question," he said, "that an Anglo-American landing in the West will take place. Such a landing is possible at any point on our extended front except in those parts bordered by submerged rocks. Two areas appear particularly favourable and therefore the most seriously threatened: the peninsulas of Cherbourg and Brest; they afford better facilities for the establishment of a bridgehead which would be methodically expanded by the employment of massive air power and heavy weapons of every kind. The enemy's main objective is to obtain a port in order to be able to land vast quantities . . . The land operation should not last more than a few hours or, in exceptional circumstances more than a few days, the attack on Dieppe being considered in this respect as an ideal case."[9]

At first Rommel had been inclined to agree with von Rundstedt on the probability of a landing in the estuary of the Somme. He discounted the Brest peninsula as being too remote for the development of subsequent operations and as possessing too few beaches for a landing. However, the more he thought about it the more convinced he became that the main blow would fall in the Baie de la Seine. The possibility of a diversionary attack on the French Mediterranean coast was not ruled out. Admiral Ruge recalls a conversation he had with him a few weeks before the invasion, when Rommel pointed to a beach on the east coast of the Cotentin Peninsula and asked whether an attack there was likely. The Admiral replied that in his view it was, at which the Field Marshal remarked, "Indeed, there they would be better protected against the westerly wind and sea."[10] This was to become Utah beach.

Admiral Krancke, Commander-in-Chief Naval Group West, thought a landing in the Scheldt more probable because of the port of Antwerp and because it offered the shortest route to the Ruhr, but he agreed that the Baie de la Seine was a possible alternative. German intelligence appears to have had little to offer in the way of a solution to this problem. Such was its state after its reorganisation following Admiral Canaris' dismissal in February 1944, that Army Group West was not allowed to work directly with it. "The natural result of such a system," said General Warlimont, "was much trouble and little intelligence."[11]

In May the anti-aircraft and anti-tank defences in the Normandy area were strengthened by Hitler's order and Rommel redistributed his reserves, moving them closer to the coast. At the same time he requested Hitler to allow the 12th SS Panzer and the Panzer Lehr divisions to be moved into the St. Lo-Carentan area, but the move was opposed by von Rundstedt and on this occasion Hitler did not support his favourite General.

So, as the decisive month of June approached there were 58 German divisions in the West, eight of which were in Holland and Belgium and the rest in France. About half of the total were of coast defence or training standard and of the 27 field divisions only ten were armoured, and three of these were in the south and one in the vicinity of Antwerp. Covering the 200 miles of the Normandy coast, six divisions were deployed, four of which were coast defence. Three of them covered the 40 mile stretch between Cherbourg and Caen and one the coast between the rivers Orne and Seine (See map).

The German coast defences comprised guns of almost every calibre from 406mm (16in) down to French 75mm (3in) field guns of World War 1. Along the Normandy coast between Cape Barfleur and Le Havre there was one battery of three 15in (38cm) guns situated 2½ miles north of Le Havre, with a range of 22 miles which dominated the eastern half of the Baie de la Seine. Along the 20 miles of coast on the east side of the Cotentin peninsula, four casemated batteries of 6.1in (155mm) guns had been erected as well as ten howitzer batteries comprising twenty-four 6in (152mm) and twenty 4.1in (104mm) guns. Along the north coast of the Baie de la Seine between Isigny and Ouistreham, a distance of 35 miles, there were only three casemated batteries of 6.1in (155mm) and one of 4.1in (104mm) guns. Between Ouistreham and the mouth of the Seine, a distance of 17 miles, three casemated batteries of 6.1in (155mm) guns and two open batteries of 5.9in (150mm) guns had been established. The beach defences in the area comprised a system of strong points at intervals of about a mile extending inland between 100 and 200 yards (90 to 180m). The casemated guns referred to were housed in concrete emplacements some 7 feet (2.1m) thick on the seaward side and on the roof. Smaller concrete gun shelters housed 50mm anti-tank guns sited to enfilade the beaches, while elaborate trench systems linked pill boxes, mortar, and machine gun posts with the crews' living quarters. Steel anti-tank wire, barbed wire and mines, as well as beach obstacles, completed the shore defences along the Baie de la Seine which, even if not as strong as Rommel would have liked were, nevertheless, to prove the most formidable the Allies had been called upon to assault.

German naval forces immediately available in the Channel area consisted of five fleet torpedo boats based on Le Havre, 23 Motor Torpedo Boats (8 of which were at Boulogne and 15 at Cherbourg), 116 minesweepers (distributed between Dunkirk and St. Malo), 44 patrol vessels, of which 21 were at Le Havre and 23 at St. Malo, and 42 artillery barges of which 16 were at Boulogne, 15 at Fecamp and 11 at Ouistream/St. Vaast. Along the Atlantic Coast between Brest and Bayonne there were five destroyers, 146 minesweepers, 59 patrol vessels and one torpedo boat. In addition 49 U-boats distributed as follows, were assigned to anti-invasion duty – Brest 24, Lorient 2, St. Nazaire 19, La Pallice 4. Of these only nine were schnorkel fitted and on the day of the invasion only 35 were ready for the sea. Although there were some 130 large ocean-going U-boats based on the Biscay ports in addition to those mentioned above, they were not considered suitable for operating in the shallow waters of the Channel and were not, therefore, included in the anti-invasion plan.

"The meagre forces at disposal of C-in-C Naval Group West," says Grand Admiral Dönitz , Commander-in-Chief of the German

9

Navy, "could not be kept permanently at sea as patrols against possible enemy landings. Since March 1944 our ships had been constantly detected by enemy radar as soon as they left harbour . . . The losses and damage sustained were so severe that even the maintenance of a permanent patrol line, let alone a reconnaissance sortie into enemy coastal waters, was out of the question."[12]

In addition to the above, six Motor Torpedo Boats, 47 Minesweepers and 13 Patrol Boats were based on Dutch and Belgian ports. The rest of the German Navy, comprising the battleship *Tirpitz* and the battle-cruiser *Scharnhorst,* both of which were seriously damaged, the pocket battleships *Admiral Scheer* and *Lutzow,* the heavy cruisers *Prinz Eugen* and *Admiral Hipper,* and the four light cruisers *Nurnberg, Leipzig, Koln* and *Emden,* together with a further 37 destroyers and 83 torpedo boats, were in either Norwegian or Baltic waters. This disposition stemmed from Hitler's fear of an Allied landing in Norway, which Churchill did his best to promote but which was firmly opposed by the British Chiefs of Staff. Dönitz was fully aware that even if he staked the entire surface force strength of his navy in one desperate throw, it was most unlikely that he could prevent the Allies from landing in France, nor effectively dispute their command of the Channel. Like Hitler, who was relying on the development of the V1 ramjet pilotless aircraft and the V2 ballistic rocket to redress a deteriorating war situation, Dönitz was pinning his faith on the employment of new weapons on which his scientists were busily working, to delay and disrupt the build-up of the Allied forces should they attempt a landing. These comprised the schnorkel fitted U-boats mentioned above, small battle units or midget submarines, long range circling torpedoes, and manned torpedoes capable of infiltrating an antisubmarine screen (*See Appendix VI).* He also had great hopes of the newly developed oyster or pressure mine (DM.Minen), which it was believed would prove unsweepable and which was being kept a closely guarded secret, by Hitler's orders, until the invasion had taken place. In the event his hopes were destined not to be fulfilled because of delays occurring in production generally, and as a result of the Führer's order that priority was to be given to the production of fighter aircraft and the repair of aircraft factories damaged as a result of Allied air attacks.

General Speidel is critical of the German Navy's part in the anti-invasion preparations. "The Navy, like the Luftwaffe," he says, "lived its own life and did not readily realise that unified command of the armed forces was urgently required."[13] It does not appear, however, that this was the fault of the Navy so much as of the system. Rommel did his best to remove the anomalies discussed above but without avail.

In sum the intended anti-invasion measures of the German Navy were:

(a) To employ U-boats, patrol craft and coast artillery to attack the landing craft.

(b) To lay large numbers of mines of all types including some of a new and simple type known as RMK or KMA mine, the whole length of the European coast.

(c) To use midget submarines and "battle" units to attack ships in the invasion area.

(d) To intensify attacks on Allied transatlantic convoys using new types of U-boats.

Production difficulties prevented this programme from being fully implemented and although mines were available in large numbers, permission to lay them was withheld.

The air situation was just as unfavourable as the naval one. The strength of the Luftwaffe had been eroded by the operations on the Russian front as well as in attempts to thwart the persistent attacks by Allied aircraft on strategic targets in Germany and the occupied countries. Luftwaffe III, assigned to the defence of the West, was commanded by Marshal Hugo Sperrle and nominally comprised some 500 aircraft, but the quality of the pilots was poor due to insufficient training. At the beginning of June 1944 only 90 bombers and 70 fighters were reported as being operational. As an example of the lack of co-ordination between the services, at this critical time the last remaining group of No.26 Fighter Geschwader was transferred to the south for a rest and out of range of the Normandy beaches. There was, as a consequence, only No. 2 Fighter Geschwader available for the defence of the area. Air reconnaissance was infrequent and inadequate. Rommel made it plain to Hitler, both in writing and by word of mouth, that an effective defence required the full co-operation of land, sea and air forces, and he pointed to the weakness of the Luftwaffe as a critical factor. "It ought to be dawning on the High Command in this fifth year of war," he is said to have told the Führer, "that the Air Force in co-operation with the Army will not only be decisive in battle but will decide the war".[14]

Notes

1   *The Halder Diaries* (English translation), Vol 4.
2   Führer Naval Conferences, September 26, 1940.
3   Ibid.
4   Dönitz, *Memoirs*
5   B. H Liddell Hart, *The Other Side of the Hill.*
6   Hans Speidel, *We Defended Normandy.*
7   The directive is reproduced in full in *Die Invasion 1944* by Percy E. Schram which is based on the War Diary of the German High Command.
8   Friedrich Ruge, *Sea Warfare 1939–1945.*
9   Friedrich Ruge, *Rommel Face au Débarquement 1944.*
10 Ibid.
11 B.H. Liddel Hart, ibid.
12 Dönitz, *Memoirs*.
13 Speidel, ibid.
14 Speidel, ibid.

Chapter Two

Planning Problems

After the fall of France in June 1940 the British Prime Minister, Mr. Churchill, issued a directive to the Chiefs of Staff enjoining them to keep harassing the enemy from the North Cape to the Spanish frontier. As a result, when the forces had been trained, various operations were undertaken such as the Vaagso raid of December 27, 1941, the highly successful attack on St. Nazaire on March 28, 1942, and the much criticised assault on Dieppe on August 19, 1942, which was referred to in the previous chapter. Of this last, Admiral of the Fleet the Earl Mountbatten of Burma said recently, "The Duke of Wellington said, 'The Battle of Waterloo was won on the beaches of Dieppe."[1] Though costly in casualties, especially amongst the Canadian troops taking part, the raid provided many lessons, the chief of which being that a frontal assault on a heavily defended port was most unlikely to succeed unless the whole area were first reduced to rubble by air and surface ship bombardment, in which case the port would be useless. Yet another result was to dampen the enthusiasm of the United States Chiefs of Staff for a return to France in 1942 with the very inadequate forces then available. Instead they lent a more receptive ear to British proposals for an invasion of North Africa which, if successful, would clear the Axis forces out of that area which could then be used as a springboard for an attack on what Churchill called 'the soft underbelly of the Axis' but which, however, proved somewhat harder than expected.

With a rapidly growing army in the United States, there was in that country a burning desire to get into action.* The US Navy was busily engaged in restoring the situation in the Pacific, and the US Army Air Corps was joining the Royal Air Force in the bombing offensive being mounted against Germany, but the Army was left spoiling for a fight. Nevertheless there was much hesitation on the part of the US Chiefs of Staff to commit their forces to the Mediterranean operation and it was only after the President came down firmly on the side of the British proposal, that planning could proceed with the first of the great amphibious operations made possible by the Allied command of the sea and for which World War II will always be remembered. The operation was given the code name 'Torch' and the planning of it was entrusted to a Flag Officer of marked ability, Vice-Admiral Sir Bertram Ramsay, who, two weeks previously, had been appointed Naval Commander, Expeditionary Force (ANCXF) with the acting rank of Admiral. Although he had been placed on the retired list in October 1938 he had been nominated for the important post of Flag Officer, Dover, in the event of war. In this appointment he had distinguished himself by organising the successful evacuation of the British Expeditionary Force from the beaches of Dunkirk in May 1940, an operation described: "As a feat of naval organisation under the stress of emergency, it has no parallel."[2] Writing to congratulate the Admiral on the KCB awarded him for the way he had conducted this most difficult task, Mr. Churchill said "The energy and the foresight called for in so formidable an undertaking and the courage required to carry it through in the teeth of the loss, gave you full opportunity to display your qualities."[3]

Ramsay installed himself with his staff in Norfolk House, London, a large red-brick building at the south-west corner of St. James's Square. In his directive dated July 9, 1942, he was made 'responsible for the general direction of all naval forces engaged in large-scale landing operations on the coast of France and the Low Countries, and the transport of the Expeditionary Force across the seas and its establishment on the enemy coast.' While it was most

* 250,860 US troops arrived in the United Kingdom during 1942 of which 153,379 travelled in British ships and 129,000 were re-embarked for North Africa. A lift of 983,000 was proposed for 1943, of which 250,000 were to arrive during the first six months.

appropriate that the man who had brought the British Army back should be the one selected to plan its return, the appointment was somewhat premature to the extent that it was not yet possible to obtain a lodgement on the coast of Europe. Even if the troops had been available there certainly were not sufficient landing craft to transport them. This directive was, therefore, temporarily put into cold storage while he turned his attention to Torch. However, in view of the size and international character which the operation had assumed and the fact that Admiral Ramsay was still a retired officer recalled for active duty, it was decided that Admiral Sir Andrew Cunningham should command the naval side of the operation. His exploits in the Mediterranean had made his name a household word on both sides of the Atlantic and he had recently been head of the British Naval Mission in Washington. Ramsay was appointed as his Deputy, a decision he loyally accepted though naturally with some disappointment.

The operation was launched on the night of November 7/8, 1942, and was an unqualified success, the Germans being taken completely by surprise. A German staff appreciation dated November 4, 1942, stated, "The relatively small number of landing craft and the fact that only two passenger ships are in this assembly at Gibraltar do not indicate any immediate landing in the Mediterranean area or on the North West African coast."[4] Many lessons were learnt from Torch and one which was to have a great bearing on future amphibious operations was the need for a very high standard of training on the part of the beach parties, without which chaos can quickly occur.

THE CASABLANCA CONFERENCE

During the time the campaign to evict the Axis forces from North Africa was in progress, a conference took place at Casablanca in January 1943, at which the President of the United States and his advisers conferred with the Prime Minister and his advisers with regard to the future conduct of the war. The author was privileged to attend this conference, during which several major decisions were taken, one of the most important being that plans for a re-entry into Europe must be initiated without further delay, and the concentration of forces and material in Britain resumed.

Lieutenant-General F.E. Morgan was selected as Chief of Staff to the Supreme Allied Commander (Designate), a title which he soon shortened to COSSAC and by which he is subsequently referred to. In his book *Overture to Overlord* he has told, with admirable clarity and wit, how he was instructed to start planning for the invasion of Europe, known as Operation Overlord. He describes the fluctuating circumstances in which that planning was carried out and which were aggravated by the delay in nominating someone to fill the post of Supreme Allied Commander.

THE COSSAC PLAN

COSSAC's first task was to select the area in France against which to launch an attack. A crucial factor in reaching a decision was the range of British fighter aircraft, so that although the Germans were occupying the west coast of Europe from the North Cape to the Spanish frontier, only the 300 miles between Flushing and Cherbourg needed to be considered. It was important that the area selected should include suitable beaches across which the assault could be made and supplies and reinforcements could be landed, as well as some ports for eventual capture. These factors limited the choice to two possible areas, the Pas de Calais between Dunkirk and the estuary of the Somme, or the Normandy coast between Caen and the Cotentin Peninsula. In the face of considerable opposition on the part of the British and American Army and Air members of the Combined Planners, who favoured the Pas de Calais, the Chiefs of Staff were persuaded by Admiral Mountbatten, in his capacity as a member of their committee and as Chief of Combined Operations, that both from a strategic as well as a naval point of view, Normandy, which he had consistently preferred, was the right choice. Intelligence showed that in the Pas de Calais area, the Germans had concentrated 25 divisions and poured untold tons of concrete into the Atlantic Wall, whereas the Normandy sector was comparatively weakly held and the Atlantic Wall was incomplete. Although the Normandy beaches were not the best available, they were adequate and sheltered from the prevailing westerly wind by the Cotentin Peninsula. Behind the beaches, the ground was suitable for the development of airfields and for the operation of tanks, despite the feature known as the Normandy 'bocage' or the presence of hedgerows.

Having decided where to attack, the next task was to ascertain the forces available and whether there were the necessary landing craft and ships to transport them across the Channel. As the American Chiefs of Staff had feared, the Mediterranean operations had absorbed a greater number of these than had been estimated, so that although Morgan had been told that a sea and air lift sufficient for five sea-borne and two air-borne divisions would be forthcoming, when he came to add up what was available he found it sufficient to lift only three sea-borne divisions and two air-borne brigades. As a result he was obliged to reduce the scale of the assault and in presenting the draft plan to the British Chiefs of Staff he stipulated that the operation would have small chance of success if the Germans were to bring more than twelve mobile divisions to bear against the beachhead within five days of the landing. He also stressed the importance of avoiding any delay in capturing a major port and of insuring against a stoppage in the landing of reinforcements and supplies due to bad weather. This was to be circumvented by the construction of two artificial ports off the beaches known as Mulberries, to be formed, it was suggested, by the sinking of the ships; the details however remained to be worked out.

When the plan came to be considered by the Combined Chiefs of Staff during the 'Quadrant' conference which took place at Quebec in August 1943, in the absence of a Supreme Commander to drive home the point that the plan "as then constituted could hardly be considered a sound operation of war,"[5] it was approved, and Morgan was instructed "to proceed with the detailed planning and full preparations". Churchill, as he has recorded,[6] suggested that every effort should be made to add at least 25 per cent to the first assault with the inevitable increase in the landing craft required, but the US Chief of Naval Operations, Fleet Admiral Ernest King, did not commit himself to making good the deficiency though he promised to consider it. "A frequent complaint against their American ally during these preparations and also of SHAEF (Supreme Headquarters Allied Expeditionary Force) against the Navy," writes Admiral Morison, "was its alleged failure to supply enough landing and beaching craft, or as it is sometimes put, starving Neptune to fatten the Pacific Fleet,"[7] and he holds the long delay on the part of the Combined Chiefs of Staff in fixing a date for the landing of the cross-Channel invasion (Overlord) as being partly responsible for the shortage. It would be pointless to resurrect this very contentious issue, but the author is convinced that the shortage of which Morgan complains so bitterly was due, not so much to the non-existence of these craft, as to their mal-distribution and the conflicting claims of the European and Pacific theatres of war. Ultimately, as will be seen, the United States provided 2,493 of the 4,126 landing ships and craft needed.

It is interesting to note that the vexed question of landing craft availability defied even Churchill's all-pervading powers of scrutiny, for on April 16, 1944, we find him complaining to the Chief of the United States Army Staff, General Marshall, "The whole of this difficult question only arises out of the absurd shortage of LSTs. How it is that the plans of two great empires like Britain and the United Sates should be so much hamstrung and limited by a hundred or two of these particular vessels will never be understood by history."[8] British ingenuity had produced the design of these specialised craft but American mass production methods alone could make them in the quantity required to meet the needs of the invasion of Normandy.

The absence of Commanders-in-Chief who would be responsible to the Supreme Commander for each of the three services, sea, land and air, was also a hindrance to the planners, despite the interim arrangements made to overcome this problem. In May 1943 the Commander-in-Chief Portsmouth, Admiral Sir Charles Little, with Commodore J. Hughes-Hallett, DSO, RN, representing him on the planning group, was made responsible for the naval side of the operation which was named 'Neptune' and with which this book is mainly concerned. Air Marshal Sir Trafford Leigh-Mallory, Commander-in-Chief, Fighter Command, similarly doubled up this duty with that of responsibility for planning the air side of the operation. He subsequently became the Air Commander-in-Chief for Overlord. Appointed as General Morgan's Deputy was Brigadier General Ray Barker, US Army, and together they laid the foundations of Anglo-United States unity amongst the planning staff, which contributed so much to the success of the whole operation. Other senior members of the team were Rear-Admiral (later Admiral of the Fleet Sir) George E. Creasy, and Captains Lyman A. Thackery and Gordon Hutchinson of the US Navy. As Morgan has recorded, some difficulty was experienced in obtaining the appointment of an integrated air staff to work with COSSAC as the Air Commands were very busily occupied with operations of their own against the enemy. Nevertheless, COSSAC's staff grew as staff always do, and by the end of 1943 amounted to 489 officers of whom 215 belonged to the US Armed Forces.

After the completion of Torch, Ramsay remained in the Mediterranean to plan the invasion of Sicily in which he took a prominent part as Naval Commander of the Eastern Task Force, and he did not return to England until August. While, as has been mentioned, the Combined Chiefs of Staff were meeting in Conference at Quebec and considering and approving the draft COSSAC plan, as well as naming a tentative date of May 1, 1944, for its execution, Ramsay took some well earned leave. He returned to Norfolk House in October and resumed his previous appointment as Naval Commander of the Expeditionary Force with Rear-Admiral George Creasy as his Chief of Staff. They had known each other before and as Ramsay himself said, "It is the first duty of an Admiral to have a good Chief of Staff;" he certainly could not have had a better or more able one. Ramsay's experience with the Mediterranean amphibious operations had taught him the futility of drawing up detailed plans for an operation, the scale of which was not known with certainty, yet this was just the situation with which he was now confronted.

APPOINTMENT OF GENERAL DWIGHT D. EISENHOWER AS SUPREME COMMANDER

After a regrettable delay and some caustic comments by Premier Stalin during the conference between the Heads of State which took place at Teheran on November 28, 1943, President Roosevelt, with Churchill's full agreement, offered the post of Supreme Commander for Operation Overlord to General Dwight D. Eisenhower. This outstanding but little known soldier had initiated the concept of an integrated Allied command under a Supreme Commander and had shown that it could be made to work. He also had a full understanding of the sea and air aspects of strategy, as well as an intimate knowledge of the complex issues, generically referred to as 'logistics', which play such a very important part in modern warfare. With the benefit of hindsight it is possible to say that no better choice could have been made. The Combined Chiefs of Staff defined his task in the following words:

"You will enter the continent of Europe and in conjunction with the other Allied Nations, undertake operations aimed at the heart of Germany and the destruction of her Armed Forces."

Amendment of the COSSAC plan

Eisenhower had in fact, seen the draft plan for Overlord in October and although not at that time personally concerned with it, had remarked that he did not consider it adequate. His appointment was dated December 6, 1943 and as soon as he had turned over his Mediterranean responsibilities to his successor, together with General Montgomery who had been nominated to command all the land forces for the invasion of Normandy, they visited Churchill who was convalescing from an attack of pneumonia at Marrakesh in Morocco. As a result of the discussion which took place there, Eisenhower, who had to fly on to the United States, instructed Montgomery on his arrival in England on January 2, 1944, to press for a revision of the plan. They both considered that the operation required to be mounted in greater strength and on a wider front and to this end they wanted an attack to be launched by two, or, if possible three, air-borne divisions instead of two air-borne brigades, to be followed by an assault from the sea of five instead of three divisions, with a floating reserve of a further two divisions for the immediate follow-up. The frontage of the landing was to be increased from 25 to 50 miles and would include beaches on the east side of the Cotentin Peninsula. Admiral Ramsay fully supported the proposed alterations to the COSSAC plan but he made it plain that he was not yet certain of being able to meet the demands of the original plan in ships and landing craft, let alone those which the revised plan of assault would require. Further, he saw little hope of acquiring them by May 1, the date planned for the assault. Ramsay and Montgomery therefore, suggested to the Supreme Commander that the operation be postponed for one month, and this the Combined Chiefs of Staff agreed to. It meant that one month's extra production of landing craft would be available and when, on March 24, the US Joint Chiefs of Staff reluctantly agreed to a postponement of the landing in the south of

France, which it had been intended to carry out simultaneously with the one in Normandy, the landing craft situation was further eased, and Ramsay's planning staff at last were able to start work on a final draft of the orders for Operation Neptune. They worked out that the revised plan postulated a requirement for 2,468 Landing Ships and Craft (*see Appendix II*). In addition 1,656 Barges, Landing Craft, Trawlers and Rhino ferries would be needed to assist in the assault and with the unloading of personnel, stores, ammunition and equipment from the larger ships which, because of their draught, would have to anchor off the beaches.

To complete the picture it was estimated that 423 Ancillary ships and craft, which included tugs and control ships for the artificial harbours which it was proposed to tow across the Channel, and 1,260 merchant ships loaded with ammunition, fuel, stores and equipment would be required for the follow-up. In all some 7,000 vessels carrying over 100,000 troops would have to be escorted across to France to arrive exactly on time, in the sequence required, at the place appointed. It was the greatest armada ever to be assembled and no British Admiral had ever before been confronted with such a formidable task.

BEACH RECONNAISSANCE

Although as we have seen, a decision had been made regarding the area in which the assault was to take place, a detailed examination of the beaches was needed before plans could be finalised. Photographic reconnaissance from the air played a great part in showing in what ways the enemy was attempting to strengthen his defences, such as by the installation of new batteries, but it was not possible to determine the composition of a beach from a photograph.

The assault area, as finally decided upon, lay on that part of the Normandy coast to the east of the Cotentin Peninsula (*see Map 2*) from a point half a mile south of Quenelle as far west as Ouistreham. It was divided into Eastern and Western sectors, the boundary line between them being drawn in a direction 025 degrees from the inshore end of the western breakwater at Port en Bessin as far as longitude 0 degrees 40′W and thence due north as far as latitude 49 degrees 40′N which formed the northern boundary of the assault area. The sectors were subdivided into assault areas as follows:

21

EASTERN SECTOR (British-Canadian)
   Gold area between Port en Bessin and Ver.
   Juno area between Ver and Langrune.
   Sword area between Langrune and Ouistreham.

WESTERN SECTOR (American)
   Utah area covering the east coast of the Cotentin Peninsula south of a point half a mile south of Quenelle to the mouth of the river Vire.
   Omaha area from the river Vire to Port en Bessin.

It was Eisenhower's intention to land a division of troops* in each of the five areas mentioned above, three being British/ Canadian and two United States, plus some Commandos and US Rangers for special duties. Two more divisions were to be at sea off the assault area to act as a floating reserve.

The eleven beaches in the Eastern sector were lettered H to R and the fourteen in the Western sector were lettered *Utah* P to W, *Omaha* A to G.

Because heavy tanks and armoured vehicles were liable to become bogged down if landed on quicksand or soft clay, it was important to obtain samples of the beaches if at all possible. The available charts based on a survey of 1896 were four years old and along such a coast, subject to the action of tidal streams and a large range of tide, considerable changes could have taken place. Although every possible scrap of information, including holiday snapshots, was collected, so important was this information that great risks were run to obtain it. Combined Operations Pilotage Parties (COPPS) comprising small numbers of naval and army officers were formed and, using both midget submarines and decked over LCPs fitted with very accurate compasses and echo-sounding gear, they operated off the enemy coast on dark nights, studying the beach gradients and underwater obstacles as well as bringing back samples of the beaches for analysis which they obtained by swimming ashore. In order not to compromise the locality of the intended landing, similar beach reconnaissances

* A British infantry Division numbered between 15 and 16 thousand, an armoured one 10 to 11 thousand. US Divisions were somewhat larger.

22

were carried out in the Pas de Calais and even off Holland. Only one party was captured, on the night of May 17/18, 1944, in the Pas de Calais area, which was fortunate to the extent that this is where it was hoped the Germans would think that the landing was going to take place. On some of the beaches, clay patches were found and, as a result, a number of tanks were fitted with rolls of steel matting, known as 'bobbins' which they laid in their path and left for other tanks following them. Then, one day in April, a wide falling bomb intended for one of the coastal batteries landed on a beach, setting off a number of explosions which indicated that land mines had been laid below High Water mark and some of them were amongst patches of clay. It was therefore decided to avoid these areas altogether and to rely on the flail tanks which had been designed to clear a path through a minefield laid in hard ground. This was only one of the many problems with which the planners had to deal during the run-up to D-day, most of which were solved thanks to the ingenuity of Major General Sir Percy Hobart and what became known as his 'Funnies'.

As a result of experience gained during the Dieppe raid, it was clear that the German shore defences could not be breached without suffering unacceptable casualties unless the infantry were given tank support from the moment of landing. From this the principle was evolved that the troops should be provided with the mechanical equipment required to overcome the obstacles which they were likely to encounter. Hobart and his staff addressed themselves to this problem and produced a remarkable variety of armoured vehicles of which the flail and bobbin tanks referred to above were a part. Others were designed to hurl explosives against beach obstructions and concrete fortifications, to carry bridges with which to span craters and anti-tank ditches, or flame throwers to deal with pill boxes. Most important of all, however, were the Duplex Drive (DD) tanks, the invention of Hungarian born Nicholas Straussler. When first demonstrated the Admiralty was sceptical of their value, but Hobart and Montgomery were enthusiastic and so was Eisenhower when he was shown them. Basically the principle was to surround a tank with a collapsible waterproof canvas screen to give it buoyancy and fit it with two propellers which, with its tracks, gave it a speed of 4.3 knots. As will be seen, this invention featured prominently in the Normandy landings.

MANPOWER

The demands of Neptune in manpower were necessarily enormous. Crews had to be found for the new landing craft and for all the many extraneous duties connected with the assault itself, such as beach and repair parties. It was estimated that 35,000 men and 10,000 women would be needed over and above the commitments involved in building up the Fleet for operations in the Far East. At this stage in the war there was a general shortage of manpower and in order to meet the above requirement the Admiralty decided to pay off four of the older battleships, five small cruisers and forty destroyers and effect other economies. Even so it was not found possible to meet all Ramsay's needs without calling on the Americans for help. Although the landing craft problem was solved after an Anglo-American conference held in London on February 13, 1944, Admiral King was not easily convinced that the battleships, cruisers and destroyers required for bombardment and fire support could not all be provided from British resources, the bone of contention being the size of the Home Fleet, standing guard over the residue of the German fleet, stationed in northern waters. However, thanks to Admiral Ramsay's persistence, and with General Eisenhower's backing, three US battleships and a destroyer were sent over in April and a division of new destroyers reached the United Kingdom a few days before D-day, so literally at the eleventh hour all the requirements for support ships were met.

TRAINING

The training given to naval and merchant navy personnel taking part in the invasion was comprehensive and included communications, assistance to embarked troops, beach organisation, and the control and direction of naval bombardment. Communications were of particular importance because, not only were British and American forces working together, but also contingents from Dominion, French, Polish, Dutch and Norwegian navies. Soldiers are unaccustomed to ships and it was most important that they should be given every assistance when embarked and shown 'the ropes'. Training facilities and assault firing areas had been allocated on the basis of the original COSSAC plan and it was not easy to expand them to meet the needs of the enlarged Eisenhower-Montgomery plan. Force 'S', which was based on the Moray Firth in northern Scotland, was handicapped by the stormy wintry weather and also by restrictions on its assault training areas. Force 'G', based on Weymouth, was not formed until March 1, 1944, and its headquarters ship, HMS *Bulolo*, did not return to the United Kingdom from the Mediterranean until April 17, but despite these difficulties, by hard work and enthusiasm, the leeway was made up. The two United States Forces 'O' and 'U', based at Portland and Plymouth respectively, did their training off the south Devonshire coast.

The realistic exercises, which formed an essential part of the training of the invasion forces, inevitably resulted in damage to many of the assault ships and craft. It is proof of the unremitting work of the repair staffs that 97.6 per cent of the British and 99.3 per cent of the United States Assault forces craft were operational on D-day.

DECEPTION AND SECURITY

Of the three elements employed to ensure the success of the invasion of Normandy, strategic deception, tactical surprise and technical ingenuity, the first named was the one to which very special attention had to be paid as without it the whole enterprise could well have been wrecked. The situation as it appeared to the enemy was described in Chapter 1. From the end of 1942 onwards Germany became increasingly anxious about the threat from the West and reports from intelligence sources left no doubt that the Allies were planning a comeback, the question was when and where? The Allies went to great trouble to keep them guessing as to their intentions. A strategic cover plan designed to conceal the state of preparedness of the invasion forces was worked out. "It boiled down to a simple policy of three points: first to postpone the date of the attack, second to indicate that the attack would come in the east rather than in the west of the threatened area, and third, after the real attack had taken place to suggest that it was only a first blow and that a second and even weightier assault would follow in the Pas de Calais area."[9] Radio played an important part in the implementation of the plan. Messages were transmitted which the Germans were sure to intercept, purporting to come from assault forces stationed in areas where none in fact were located. These culminated in a bogus large scale harbour exercise on the day before the assault although the forces had in fact sailed. Radar counter-measures were used to jam enemy radar stations and 'window' was dropped by aircraft to simulate the movements of large convoys of ships on the enemy's radar screens.

Sir John Masterman also says: "When participating in the deception for Overlord, we reaped the full advantage of having the German intelligence service here (UK) under our control," and he goes on to say, "we were able to state with confidence what the Germans did *not* know about our preparations as well as what they did know,"[10] and one of those things about which the enemy had little or no information was the artificial harbours (Mulberries). However it was not possible to keep from him knowledge of the security arrangements which it was necessary to take as the date of the invasion approached. For instance on February 9, 1944, all civilian travel between Britain and Eire was suspended in order to prevent information reaching the numerous German agents stationed in Dublin. On April 17 an unprecedented step was taken when diplomatic privileges were curtailed and the movements of foreign diplomats or their couriers into or out of the United Kingdom was prohibited. The censorship of correspondence was also extended. By and large the strategic deception plan worked well and even after the invasion had taken place the enemy continued in his belief that the real assault would come in the Pas de Calais area.

However, just as in January 1940 the Allies failed to make use of a piece of vital information which fell into their hands, warning them of Germany's plan for the invasion of the Low Countries and France,[11] so four and a half years later did the Germans fail to heed a similar piece of intelligence. The message by which the BBC was to warn the French Resistance of the imminence of the invasion became known to the Abwehr, the German counter-intelligence service. When it was transmitted on June 1, 2 and 3, and the information passed by the Abwehr on the evening of June 3 to all military commanders in Belgium and France, almost no notice was taken of it, one of von Rundstedt's staff officers being quoted as saying: "As if Eisenhower would announce the invasion over the BBC!"[12]

Notes

1 "Dieppe 1942", BBC Documentary 2125, August 22, 1972.
2 L.F. Ellis, *Official Military History of World War II.*
3 W.S. Chalmers, *Full Cycle.*
4 Ibid.
5 Montgomery of Alamein, *Normandy to the Baltic.*
6 Churchill, *The Second World War,* Vol V.
7 Samuel Morison, *History of US Naval Operations in World War II,* Vol XI.
8 Churchill, ibid.
9 J.C. Masterman, *The Double Cross System.*
10 Ibid.
11 See *Belgium 1939–1940,* official publication of the Belgium Ministry of Foreign Affairs.
12 Paul Carrell, *Invasion – They're Coming.*

Chapter Three

The Naval Plan

In traditional terms the task confronting the naval planners was to organise the safe and timely arrival of the troop convoys required for an assault on a hostile shore. Secondly the plan must provide for the landing of reinforcements without interruption and at as high a rate as possible, for five to six weeks after the landing had taken place. Air reconnaissance and intelligence had provided them with a fairly accurate estimate of the enemy's strength and capabilities as given in Chapter 1. The naval threat, while not particularly formidable as compared with the strength of the Allied forces, could not by any means be ignored. At the same time British naval resources were by now fully extended and Ramsay appreciated that he must keep his demands down to what was essential. It had been agreed at the conference between President Roosevelt and Mr. Churchill at Cairo in November 1942 that the British, Dominion and Allied Navies, excluding that of the United States, should provide all the naval forces needed for Neptune, but after the increase in the weight of the assault demanded by General Eisenhower, it was clear that the US Navy would have to be asked to contribute. The preliminary estimate of the naval forces needed, based on the original COSSAC plan, totalled 467 warships and this the Admiralty considered far too many! Now the estimate, based on the revised plan, totalled 702, but Ramsay was fully able to justify his demands and in the end his figure was accepted and it was agreed that the US Navy be asked to assist. As has been related, this Admiral King agreed to do, once he was satisfied that the requirement could not be met from British resources. In general terms the demand was for battleships, monitors, cruisers and destroyers to engage and neutralise the enemy coast defences while the landing was in progress and to support the assault as required by the army subsequently. Frigates, destroyer escorts and corvettes were needed to provide protection to the convoys on the passage across the Channel, and patrol and coastal craft to ward off attacks by enemy 'E' boats and 'battle' weapons, and also low-flying aircraft.

THE COMMAND SYSTEM

Ramsay was anxious to make as much use as possible of the existing system of command, rather than create a new one. He was, of course, junior to the three Commanders in Chief of the Home Ports chiefly concerned, the Nore, Portsmouth and Plymouth, but once the invasion was launched, all the naval forces involved would come under his direct command. He gave careful consideration to this problem, but such was the spirit of co-operation amongst all concerned with this great enterprise that no difficulties arose on this score and co-ordination between the commands was excellent.

The command system for the assault and follow-up convoys was as follows:

EASTERN SECTOR
Naval Commander Eastern Task Force (NCETF) Rear-Admiral Sir Philip Vian: flagship HMS *Scylla*

FORCE S (SWORD)
Rear-Admiral Arthur G. Talbot – HMS *Largs* (3rd British Infantry Division and 27th Armoured Brigade)

FORCE G (GOLD)
Commodore C.E. Douglas-Pennant, RN – HMS *Bulolo* (50th British Infantry Division and 8th Armoured Brigade)

FORCE J (JUNO)
Commodore G.N. Oliver, RN – HMS *Hilary* (3rd Canadian Infantry Division and 2nd Canadian Armoured Brigade)

FOLLOW-UP FORCE L

Rear-Admiral W.E. Parry – HMS *Albatross* (7th Armoured Division and 49th Infantry Division; 4th Armoured Brigade and 51st Highland Division)

WESTERN SECTOR

Naval Commander Western Task Force (NCWTF) Rear-Admiral Alan G. Kirk, USN – flagship USS *Augusta*

FORCE O (OMAHA)

Rear-Admiral J.L. Hall, USN – *Ancon* (1st Division and part of 29th Division US Army)

FORCE U (UTAH)

Rear-Admiral Don P. Moon, USN – USS *Bayfield* (4th Division US Army)

FOLLOW-UP FORCE B

Commodore C.D. Edgar, USN – USS *Maloy* (2nd, 9th, 79th, 90th and remainder of 29th Division US Army)

The Naval Commander of each Naval Task and Assault Force remained in command until the Army was firmly established ashore.

Amongst the ships detailed for bombardment in the Eastern Sector were Rear-Admirals F. H. G. Dalrymple-Hamilton and W. R. Patterson commanding the 2nd and 10th Cruiser squadrons respectively. Although senior to the Task Force and Assault Commander they agreed to waive their seniority and act under the latter's instructions. A similar situation existed in the Western Sector and was solved equally satisfactorily. Rear-Admiral Jaujard of the Free French Navy, who had hoisted his flag in the cruiser *Georges Leygues,* also agreed to be omitted from the chain of command.

MINESWEEPING

The minesweeping requirement was not included in the warship total given at the beginning of the chapter, but of its importance there was no question. The existence of minefields the whole length of the Channel south of latitude 50 degrees N to within ten miles of the French coast was well established. South of the minefields lay a channel used by the Germans for coastal traffic and this might reasonably be expected to be clear unless at the last moment the enemy decided to mine it. It was decided, therefore, to site the lowering positions for the Landing Ships Infantry (Large) within this channel. Inshore of the coastal channel it was suspected that ground mines might be laid and the area would need to be cleared to allow access to the beaches and freedom of movement for the bombarding ships. The minesweeping plan adopted was as follows:

(a) Two channels were to be cut through the mine barrier for each assault force, a fleet minesweeping flotilla being employed for each channel.

(b) Clear areas inshore of the coastal channel were to be established as needed for bombardment, etc.

(c) As soon as possible the approach channels were to be widened to give more sea room.

(d) After the assault, mines subsequently laid by the enemy to be swept.

The cutting of the approach channels called for the largest single minesweeping operation ever undertaken in war and 255 sweepers and dan layers were required for it. Each channel was buoyed at intervals of a mile with lighted dan buoys, and accurate navigation was essential. As the sweepers would be sweeping across a tidal stream varying in strength and direction from hour to hour, course had to be adjusted accordingly and at one period it was necessary to change the side of the sweep from port to starboard. An experienced minesweeping officer was made responsible for minesweeping in each area. As the channels would be in use for some weeks after the landing, arrangements were made for Trinity House to replace the dan buoys by ocean light buoys.

If it was not only off the Normandy coast that the mining threat existed, for in the six weeks preceding the invasion the enemy had stepped up is aerial minelaying off the south coast ports where he could see shipping was being assembled, so the approaches to these had also to be kept clear. Fortunately, due to the Allied air superiority, the minelaying was confined to moonless nights; also, despite the tempting targets presented by the dense assemblies of shipping, bombing attacks on them were few and of little consequence.

BEACH DEFENCES

While Ramsay hoped he could count on adequate naval support and overwhelming air superiority to protect his convoys on their passage across the Channel, after the mine threat, which gave him greatest concern, were the underwater obstacles which the enemy was busily planting on the very beaches selected for the landing. It seemed as if he had been given the tip-off, but as we now know this was not the case, but merely the result of Rommel's drive and initiative. As the obstacles grew in quantity it became obvious that a landing during darkness would involve too great a risk and that in any case, demolition squads would have to be landed close behind the infantry to clear them. From the soldier's point of view it was desirable to land at high tide so that the distance which the infantry would have to cover to reach the enemy's defences would be as short as possible. However, at high tide the obstacles would be covered but not sufficiently to prevent damage to any landing craft which struck them, hence from the naval point of view, a landing at low tide was preferable. The rise and fall of the tide off the Normandy coast is of the order of 25 feet at Springs and 19 feet at Neaps and, the beaches being gently shelving with a gradient of between 1 in 100 to 1 in 200, there was thus a long stretch of shore uncovered at low water. Ramsay discussed this knotty problem with Montgomery and a compromise solution was reached by which the landing would be made at half tide, i.e. between three and four hours before high water, to give the demolition parties a chance to deal with the obstacles before the second wave of assault troops landed and the rising tide put a stop to their work. For his part, Montgomery decided that, to minimise the risk of heavy casualties amongst the infantry as they crossed the open beach, the first wave should consist of waterproofed tanks (DD tanks), followed by specialised armour, and then the infantry. This was a wise decision which paid a good dividend.

BEACH ORGANISATION

An efficient beach organisation, as the Mediterranean operations had shown, was essential to control the movements of landing craft, coasters, ferries and vehicles, as well as to prevent the accumulation of dumps of stores. As Ramsay was to say in his report on the operation, "The task that confronts beachmasters on first landing is superhuman. The beaches are long and difficult to inspect quickly or easily at all. The beach parties . . . are extremely vulnerable. Things are happening very quickly on all sides." The plan, therefore, provided for two authorities to be established on the far shore, viz:

(a)   The Beach Naval Officer in Charge (NOIC) who would be the naval executive authority on his beach and directly responsible to the Assault Force Commanders.

(b)   The Senior Officer Ferry Craft (SOFC) who, working in close co-operation with the Principal Beach Master and the Beach Group Commander, was responsible for the control of all the ferry craft operating off his beach.

At a meeting convened by the War Office it had been agreed that the control of all ferry craft should be exercised by the Navy to meet the Army's wishes and that there should be maximum inter-service representation at all levels.

The reception of shipping and convoys arriving in the assault area and the assembly and sailing of return convoys were made the responsibility of two authorities afloat in each area known as Captain Southbound Sailings and Captain Northbound Sailings.

BOMBARDMENT

It was decided to rely on a combination of air bombing and naval bombardment to soften up the enemy's defences in the assault area, details of which were given in Chapter 1. The three Commanders in Chief drew up a joint plan for this, which specified:

(a)   The batteries to be bombed prior to the day of the assault (D-day), which were those such as the 15in guns north of Le Havre and the 6in batteries on the Cotentin Peninsula, which could be of particular nuisance to the assault forces. However, in order not to disclose the assault area, batteries elsewhere would have to be bombed at the same time and this would reduce the weight of the attack on the real targets.

(b) The ten batteries to be bombed on the night preceding D-day, on each of which it was planned to drop 100 tons of bombs. Four of these were in the British sector.

(c) The six batteries, three in each sector, which were to be bombed by medium bombers during the two hours prior to the assault.

(d) The batteries which were to be engaged by naval gunfire during the assault.

(e) The heavy and medium bomber effort in support of the drenching fire against the beach defences, which was the task of the smaller warships and gun support craft.

The aim was the neutralisation of all batteries capable of interfering with the assault. Fighter aircraft, the pilots of which had received special training, were allotted to the bombarding forces for periods of 35 to 45 minutes on specified targets as well as for impromptu shoots throughout the day. After the batteries were silenced and/or captured, the ships' guns were at the disposal of the army for engaging mobile batteries, counter-attacking enemy formations and any other tasks which would help the troops to gain their objectives. In all 106 warships, excluding LCT (G)s and LCT (R)s were detailed for bombardment as follows:

	RN and RCN	USN	French and Dutch
Battleships	3	3	–
Monitors	2	–	–
Cruisers	17	3	3
Destroyers	37	31	5
Gunboats	–	–	2

The distribution was 73 in the Eastern sector and 33 in the Western. The bombarding ships were expected to use a lot of ammunition so special arrangements were made to have lighters loaded with outfits of ammunition for the various ships and on return to

34

harbour, these could be placed alongside immediately, thus enabling the ship to return to her bombarding position with the minimum of delay. Further, it was recognised that there would be instances when the guns themselves would need to be replaced through reaching the life given to the barrel. In the case of 6 inch guns and below, a stock was piled at the southern dockyard ports, but ships requiring to replace a 15 inch gun would have to fetch it from the north of England.

LOADING AND ASSEMBLY

In the United Kingdom the major problems were the assembly of the various convoys and the training of personnel, the second being of the utmost importance. Every step required close co-ordination between the services. For example, the Army had concentrated troops, stores and equipment in camps and dumps throughout the country. These had to be moved to areas close to the selected ports of embarkation. The troops were divided between those chosen for the assault, the floating reserve and the follow-up, and the Navy had to organise its convoys accordingly, make the necessary landing ships and craft available, and arrange for them to be sailed to the assembly anchorages and thence to arrive in their proper sequence on time at the right beach.

Once the place and scale of the assault had been settled, the Army could produce its 'Q' appreciation. This gave the detailed requirements of the invading forces in troops, tanks, vehicles, equipment, ammunition, stores, rations, in fact everything the fighting soldier was likely to need on the far shore. These had to be tactically loaded so what would be needed first was loaded last. The loading problem was to some extent simplified by the construction and use of 55 concrete hards or roadways sloping down into the water, against which a landing ship or craft could nose and lower her ramp, thus enabling tanks, armoured vehicles and trucks to be driven straight on board.

It was necessary to set out the plan for the loading and assembly of the various forces in great detail, but the following is a summary of the orders issued, from which it can be seen that use had to be made of every available port and harbour in the south of England. Letters were assigned to the forces corresponding to the five areas

Juno, Gold, Sword, Omaha and *Utah* in which they were to land, except Forces 'B' and 'L' which were the follow-up forces for the Western and Eastern sectors respectively.

	Force	Loading ports	Assembly ports
	'J'	Southampton and Portsmouth	Southampton, Solent, Spithead
	'G'	Southampton	Southampton, Solent, Spithead
2 Brigade Groups	'S'	Portsmouth	Portsmouth, Spithead
1 Brigade Group	'S'	Newhaven, Shoreham	Newhaven, Shoreham
	'O'	Weymouth, Portland	Weymouth, Portland, Poole
1 R.C.T. *	'U'	Torquay, Brixham, Dartmouth East	Torbay, Brixham, Dartmouth
1 R.C.T.	'U'	Dartmouth West	Dartmouth
1 R.C.T.	'U'	Plymouth East	Salcombe
1 R.C.T.	'B'	Plymouth West	Plymouth
2 R.C.T.	'B'	Falmouth	Falmouth, Helford River, Fowey
1 Brigade Group	'L'	Tilbury	Southend, Sheerness
2 Brigade Groups	'L'	Felixstowe	Harwich
1st US Build Up Div.		Bristol Channel ports	British Channel ports

* Regimental Combat Team approximately equivalent to a Brigade.

MERCHANT VESSELS

Type	Loading ports	Assembly ports
Stores coasters	Thames 89	Thames 68
	Grimsby 12	Solent 55
	Bristol Channel 104	Bristol Channel 82
MT Ships	London, Tilbury 37,	London, Southend,
	Bristol Channel 37	Bristol Channel
Personnel Ships	Tilbury 6	Tilbury
	Bristol Channel 9	Bristol Channel

ATTACHED FORCES

Force	Assembly ports
Covering Force Destroyers	Plymouth and Portsmouth
Coastal Forces	Dartmouth, Portland, Newhaven and Dover

Ferry Service Landing craft	Chichester, Langston Harbour and Poole
Tugs, Salvage vessels and Accommodation ships	Ports between Falmouth and Southend
Escort vessels and mine-sweepers	With the convoys to which they were attached.
Bombarding ships, Eastern sector	Clyde
Bombarding ships, Western sector	Belfast
Blockships	Oban

With so many merchant ships taking part in the assault and the build-up, the Ministry of War Transport felt obliged to make it clear to the crews the risks involved and officers and men were invited to sign on for invasion duties in what became known as 'V' (Volunteer) scheme. It is a tribute to the devotion to duty of these men that with very few exceptions, and those mostly for reasons of age, health or family, the great majority welcomed the opportunity of adding to the laurels they had already won in the Battle of the Atlantic. As has been mentioned, merchant shipping was the keystone of the arch on which the Cross Channel operation was built, and it was not only the big ships loaded with the sinews of war which made possible the operation, but, "Coasters which had never carried anything more exciting than coal or potatoes between Liverpool and Ireland found themselves working under the hallmark of adventure, Combined Operations, carrying out beaching exercises and learning to beach without broaching to."[1] The work of these small ships was invaluable as, ton for deadweight ton, in a given time they could put ashore almost twice the amount of stores, especially ammunition and petrol, as the big ships.

BUILD-UP AND TURN-ROUND CONTROLS

The importance of speed and quantity in the 'build-up' following the assault has been stressed and to ensure as far as possible against unnecessary delay, Admiral Ramsay set up two interservice organisations, one the 'Build-Up Control' known as BUCO and the other the 'Turn-Round Control' known as TURCO. While BUCO dealt with the problems arising from meeting the needs of the Army with the shipping available, TURCO organised the movements of ships between the ports, where berths and cargoes were available, and the beachhead, and saw to it that unloaded ships returned to reload as rapidly as possible. Simplification was the keynote of both these organisations and to this end every ship was ordered to carry on her bridge a large blackboard on which bold letters were painted to indicate her country of departure, the area in the United Kingdom from which she came or to which she was bound, the type of cargo carried and the number of the convoy to which she had been allocated. Thus a board marked F W P 3 indicated a ship from France bound for the Isle of Wight area belonging to personnel convoy number 3. The escort commander steaming through a crowded anchorage could thus easily pick out the ships of the convoy under his orders.

THE MULBERRIES

Mention has been made of the artificial harbours which it was intended to tow across the Channel and position off the Normandy beaches. Mr. Churchill has been credited with originating the idea in a paper which he wrote for the War Cabinet in 1917, but General Eisenhower has recorded[2] that he first heard of it from Admiral Mountbatten at a conference in the spring of 1942 when it was received with considerable scepticism. Mountbatten, however, persevered with it and ultimately persuaded Churchill to give it his blessing. It was rightly surmised, and experience in Italy had confirmed it, that before abandoning a port the Germans would sabotage it so thoroughly that extensive salvage operations would be required before it could be used. As the whole success of the assault depended on the ability of the Allies to build up their forces more rapidly than the enemy could reinforce his, it was imperative that this part of the operation should not be at the mercy of the weather which, at any time of the year, is notoriously unreliable in the Channel, even in summer.

The Combined Chiefs of Staff had approved the idea of the artificial harbours during their meeting at Quebec, but at that time, the details of their construction and assembly had not been worked out. It was January 1944 before the plans were ready and construction could begin. Because of the need for secrecy they were given the code name of Mulberries and the first plans were prepared by the War Office which controlled the use of concrete.

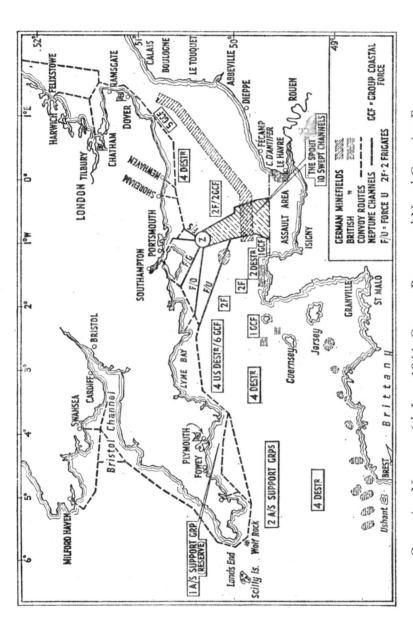

Operation Neptune, 6th June 1944. Convoy Routes and Naval Covering Forces.

However, as Admiral Ramsay has recorded, "It was apparent soon after taking up my appointment that much greater supervision of the preparations and an experienced naval staff to control the operation was necessary."[3] He secured the appointment of Rear-Admiral W. G. Tennant, CB, a flag officer of marked ability who had been in charge of the Dunkirk evacuation on the French coast, to take charge of the Mulberry operation and also of the petrol supply organisation known as 'Pluto' (Pipe Line under the ocean) which is discussed later. However, Admiral Ramsay made no secret of his lack of enthusiasm for both these projects which he regarded as complicating his job in getting the invasion fleet safely across to the shores of France. Yet, as will be related, during the agonising four days when, due to bad weather, the success or failure of the operation precariously hung in the balance, it was the Arromanches Mulberry which saved the day.

The main components of the Mulberries, two of which were to be assembled, comprised 146 concrete caissons known as 'Phoenixes', each 200 feet (61m) long but of varying sizes according to the depth of water in which they were to be sunk. The largest displaced 6,044 tons and the smallest 1,672 tons and their construction required 330,000 cubic yards (252,310 cubic metres) of concrete and 31,000 tons of steel. They were fitted with buoyancy chambers which could be flooded, thus enabling them to be sunk in the appointed place in a matter of fifteen to twenty minutes. Since time was of the essence and there were insufficient docks and slipways on which they could be built, having regard to all other urgent shipbuilding and repair work in hand, recourse was had to the excavation of twelve deep pits close to the Thames in which the bottom section could be built and then floated out to be completed afloat. A total of 48 caissons were constructed in this way, 57 in dry docks, 18 in two wet docks and 23 on slipways.

On taking up his appointment, Tennant expressed doubt regarding the ability of the Mulberries to withstand even a moderate gale and estimated that it would take two weeks to place them. He proposed that 70 obsolete ships be prepared as blockships and sunk as soon as possible after the assault had taken place to afford some shelter to the landing beaches before the Phoenix breakwaters could be assembled. The 59 blockships, known as 'Gooseberries', provided 24,000 feet (7,115m) of breakwater and saved the situation when the great gale occurred two weeks after the landing. It was also decided to moor a number of 200 feet long floating cruciform steel structures known as 'Bombardons', secured end to end, to provide some shelter to a deep water anchorage which was to be established to seaward of the Phoenix breakwater. Within the artificial harbour, floating piers and pier-heads known as 'Whales' and 'Beetles', able to rise and fall with the tide, were to be established to enable coasters as well as LSTs and LCTs to discharge direct to the shore. The pierheads consisted of steel pontoons, 200ft long and 60ft beam, secured between piles driven into the seabed between which they rose and fell. They contained generating sets, crew accommodation and storage space, and were fitted with a sloping ramp against which a landing craft could berth head on and, by lowering her ramp, vehicles could drive off and along the floating roadway to the beach. Elsewhere coasters could berth on the pontoons and discharge into trucks. Four Whale units were allotted to each Mulberry and the longest of the floating piers was just over half a mile in length. Assembly ports for the Mulberry units were assigned as follows:

Phoenixes	Selsey, Dungeness and Thames
Bombardons	Portland
Whales	Solent and Selsey
Tugs	Portland and Spithead

PLUTO

The modern mechanised army is a great devourer of fuel and its supply in sufficient quantity to the armies once they were ashore, presented a special problem which would become of increasing importance as they advanced. The problem was solved in two ways:

(a) Four pipelines known as 'Tombola' (6in) (15cm) and 'Amethea' (10in) (25cm) would be laid, two in each sector, from the shore to offshore moorings to which a large tanker could secure. After connecting her hose to the end of the pipeline attached to the mooring, she could discharge to the shore at a rate of 600 tons per hour.

41

(b) Ten pipelines would be laid across the English Channel from Sandown Bay, Isle of Wight, to Querqueville, to the west of Cherbourg. They were of two kinds (i) 'HAIS', a flexible pipe similar to an electric cable without the core which could be laid by a cable ship and (ii) 'HAMEL', a flexible steel pipe wound on to floating drums, 50 feet in diameter, from which it unreeled as they were towed along.

COMBINED REPAIR ORGANISATION AND TUG CONTROL

Two other organisations were created as part of the Neptune plan, one known as Combined Operations Repair Organisation (COREP) and the other as Tug Control (COTUG). The first was set up by the Admiralty to co-ordinate the work of repair to ships and landing craft damaged during the assault and to provide maintenance facilities. Every dock, slipway, repair berth and workshop facility, whether belonging to a naval dockyard or a private firm, was placed under their control and the maintenance of the invasion fleet was given priority over all other work. The plan also created an extraordinary demand for tugs far in excess of those available in the United Kingdom. The Mulberry operations alone required 35 heavy tows daily for over two weeks and there were many others of a lighter kind. Even though an emergency tug-building programme had been initiated on both sides of the Atlantic, a full requirement was not met by the time the invasion was launched and the shortage was particularly felt by the Salvage organisation. In all 132 tugs of varying size from ocean-going to those normally employed on river and harbour work were employed. Despite the variety of flags under which they sailed this fleet of tugs rendered yeoman service and the COTUG organisation ensured their most economical employment. The COREP and COTUG organisations had to work in close co-operation with each other and with the salvage organisation, which was in the charge of Commodore T. McKenzie, RNVR, of Metal Industries Ltd. who had been responsible for raising the ships of the German Navy, scuttled in Scapa Flow after World War I. His organisation amply proved its worth, especially during the period following the great gale already referred to.

INTERDICTION OF ENEMY TRANSPORTATION

Although not strictly a naval problem, mention must be made of an operation which made a major contribution to the success of the Normandy invasion. As has been stated the success or failure of the operation depended largely on the rate of build-up of the Allied Forces in the bridgehead exceeding that of the enemy. The Germans possessed interior lines of communication in the form of a network of roads and railways which, unless interdicted, would undoubtedly give them a great advantage in this respect over the sea-borne lines of communication on which the Allies had to depend.

As a result of experience gained in the Middle East and in Sicily, Professor (now Lord) Zuckerman drew up what became known as the Transportation Plan in preparation for the Normandy invasion. It had the full support of General Eisenhower and of his deputy, Air Chief Marshal Sir Arthur Tedder. It called for a 90-day attack against 72 carefully chosen targets, 39 of which were in Germany and 33 in France and Belgium. The plan was opposed by Air Chief Marshal Sir Arthur Harris, Commander-in-Chief, Bomber Command and General Carl Spaatz, Commanding General, US Strategic Air Force, both of whom were reluctant to abandon their planned bombing programmes. They did not believe that railway centres, including major junctions, marshalling yards and rolling stock could be hit with the accuracy required or that attacks on them would produce the reaction on the part of the enemy necessary to reduce the strength of his still formidable fighter squadrons. A high level controversy ensued which had to be carried to the President-Prime Minister level before it could be resolved. Roosevelt fully supported Eisenhower and Tedder, and Churchill, who had supported Harris, reluctantly acquiesced. With considerable misgivings Harris and Spaatz carried out their part of the plan, although the latter still gave preference to his oil targets, but the combined effect was successful beyond anyone's hopes. In the four months prior to D-day, 76,200 tons of bombs were dropped on 80 road and rail targets with the result that by D-day 75 per cent of the rolling stock within 150 miles of the Normandy beachhead was unusable, while the whole railway system of north-west Europe had been severely dislocated. Every bridge serving the battlefield was down and more than 5,000 enemy aircraft had been destroyed in combat. This achievement prevented serious interference by the Luftwaffe in the preparations for the invasion and also effectively reduced the enemy's ability to reinforce the threatened area whilst the Allies were building up their strength.

Notes
1   J.L. Hodson, *British Merchantmen at War.*
2   Eisenhower, *Crusade in Europe.*
3   ANCXF Report on Neptune, Vol 1.

Chapter Four

Final Preparations

On April 2, 1944, Admiral Ramsay issued a provisional copy of his orders for Operation Neptune to certain selected authorities. In view of their complexity they were arranged chronologically and not separately for each force and they were necessarily voluminous, totalling more than 1,000 pages of typescript. This fact occasioned some comment amongst the US members of the staff. "The planning methods of the two navies were also very different," writes Admiral Morison. "The British were accustomed to making detailed plans at top level; the Americans to issuing broad directives to lower echelons who were encouraged to work out their own details."[1] But this was no ordinary operation and when it is remembered that the movements of every one of the several thousand ships involved had to be co-ordinated and linked to a timetable, and that it was essential for each to know what the other was doing, then it seems that no other system would have worked, since nothing could be left to chance or individual whim.

The orders went to the printers on April 10; two weeks later they were distributed and a limited number of authorities were instructed to open them, the risk to security thus entailed being considered acceptable. It was appreciated that the Commanding Officers of some of the smaller ships taking part might be overwhelmed when in due course they were ordered to open their copies of the orders, hence arrangements were made for them to be briefed by staff officers familiar with the contents.

Move to Battle Headquarters

On April 26 Admiral Ramsay and his staff moved from London to their Battle Headquarters at Southwick House in the middle of the operation area. This early Victorian mansion, nine miles from Portsmouth and lying in a park of some 360 acres behind Portsdown Hill, had been requisitioned a few months previously to house the Navigation and Fighter Direction School which had been bombed out of its home in the dockyard. The author had just assumed command of the establishment when, in January 1944, he was visited by General de Guingand, Chief of Staff to General Montgomery, who informed him that he had been charged with finding a suitable headquarters from which to launch the invasion. After the General had seen the facilities available in the park and the house he expressed himself satisfied that it was an ideal situation, especially as the Army units would not be arriving until the trees came into leaf and there would then be ample cover in the woods for their tents and caravans. It was agreed that Admiral Ramsay and the Naval Staff who would arrive first, should occupy the house, while the Supreme Commander, General Eisenhower, and his staff, together with General Montgomery and the staff of 21 Army Group, would be accommodated in the park. In March the Navigation School was transferred to the RN College, Greenwich, though the Fighter Direction School remained, and work went ahead with the conversion of the rest of the establishment into a Battle Headquarters. This involved the requisitioning of local houses as WRNS Quarters, the laying of power cables and teleprinter lines, the erection of numerous Nissen huts and even the sinking of a well to augment the inadequate water supply. Hardly a day passed but some new requirement had to be met but, with the willing co-operation of all concerned, when the Commander-in-Chief arrived and his flag was broken at the head of the flagstaff specially erected for the purpose outside the front porch, all was ready. The long drawing room, panelled with mirrors, had been converted into an operations room and covering the east wall was a huge relief map of the invasion area and the English Channel. To safeguard this secret, all the windows of the room had been completely blacked out and only Commanders in Chief and their Staff and Wren

Left: Vice Admiral Lord Louis Mountbatten, Chief of Combined Operations, who initiated the procurement of Landing Craft. /*Imperial War Museum*

Below: Admiral Sir Bertram Ramsay and General Dwight D. Eisenhower outside the entrance to Southwick House. /*IWM*

Left: Air Chief Marshal Sir Trafford Leigh Mallory, Air Officer Commanding in Chief Allied Air Forces for Operation Neptune. */IWM*

Below: Rear Admiral Alan G. Kirk, USN, commanding the Western Naval Task Force, with General Omar M. Bradley, Commanding General US First Army. */IWM*

Right: Admiral Sir Bertram Ramsay in conversation with his Chief of Staff, Rear Admiral G. E. Creasy (left) and Rear Admiral Sir Philip Vian (right). */IWM*

Bottom right: Rear Admiral Sir Philip Vian, commanding the Eastern Naval Task Force, in conversation with Commodore 1st Class G. N. Oliver, Naval Commander Force J. */IWM*

Right: Field Marshal Erwin
Rommel, Inspector General
of Coast Defences and
Commander Army Group B,
with his naval adviser Vice
Admiral Friedrich Ruge.
/Courtesy Adm. Ruge

Below: Southwick House,
Near Portsmouth.
Headquarters from which
Operation Neptune was
launched. */RN Official*

Top: The erection of beach defences by the Germans off the French coast is interrupted by Allied aircraft. /IWM

Above: HMCS *Prince David* – Landing Ship Infantry (Medium) attached to Force J. /IWM

Top: Landing Ship Tank. /*IWM*

Above: Landing Craft (Flak). Converted LCT fitted with A/A
guns to provide A/A protection to assault forces. /*IWM*

Top: Landing Craft Gun (large). Converted LCT mounting two
4.7in guns to provide close support for assault troops. /*IWM*

Above: Harbour Defence Motor Launches preceding Bangor
class minesweepers used to sweep channels for the invasion forces
through the German mined area off France. /*IWM*

Officers acting as plotters, had access to it. The map had been erected some days previously by a dockyard carpenter, who arrived with it in sections wrapped in black hessian in a small RN van, and this white-haired little man had been entrusted with one of the most closely guarded secrets of all time.

The stage for Operation Neptune was set, but as yet neither D-day nor H-hour, the date and time when the first troops would land on the beaches, had been decided. It had been agreed that the landings should take place between 12 minutes before and 90 minutes after sunrise, and three to four hours before High Water; also there had to be moonlight during the night before for the paratroops which were due to begin landing soon after midnight. These requirements limited the choice of days during the month of June to 5 to 7, or 18 to 20, with a strong preference for the earlier period. As the time of High Water at the various beaches varied by as much as one and a quarter hours, the earliest being at *Utah* and *Omaha*, it was not possible to synchronise H-hour for the five assault forces. On May 1 a meeting took place at Supreme Headquarters at which the situation revealed by the latest air photographs of the beaches was considered. These showed that the enemy was pushing his lines of beach obstacles farther out to sea and, as Ramsay insisted that they must be dealt with when they stood in not more than two feet of water, this involved an adjustment of H-hour and gave added preference to June 5 and 6 with June 7 only acceptable in case of absolute necessity. In the event, due to a 24 hours' postponement, further adjustment of the H-hours was necessary, and those finally decided upon were:

Utah and *Omaha* beaches 0630   *Gold* beach 0725
Juno beach 0735–0745   *Sword* beach 0725

The provisional fixing of D-day somewhat in advance of the actual assault was necessary because sailing orders had to be issued to some of the blockships anchored off Oban by D minus 8 days. At the same time provision was made in case the weather on the day selected proved unsuitable and ships were required to reverse course and put into emergency ports.

EXERCISE 'FABIUS'

A final rehearsal of the part Forces 'O', 'S', 'J', and 'G' were to play in the assault took place in the English Channel between May 2 and 6. The exercise, known as 'Fabius', was made as realistic as possible and involved a landing by Force 'O' on Slapton Sands, by Force 'S' to the west of Littlehampton, by Force 'J' at Bracklesham Bay , and by Force 'G' at Hayling Island. The Portsmouth and Plymouth commands provided covering forces to the southward in case the enemy tried to interfere with the exercise. A week previously Force 'U' had carried out a similar final rehearsal on Slapton Sands and, while on passage from its base at Portland, had encountered a group of nine enemy 'E' boats which succeeded in sinking two tank landing craft and damaging a third with a loss of 638 officers and men, 441 of which were soldiers. These casualties were higher than the force was to suffer during the actual landing. Admiral King ordered the losses to be made good by the transfer of replacements from the Mediterranean.

On May 15 an historic conference took place at General Montgomery's Headquarters in St. Paul's School, London, which he had attended as a boy. Present on this occasion were HM King George VI, the Prime Minister Mr. Churchill, Field Marshal Jan Smuts, the British Chiefs of Staff, the Supreme Commander, the Commanders-in-Chief of the three services and all the Force Commanders concerned. The proceedings were opened by General Eisenhower who was followed by Ramsay, Montgomery and Leigh-Mallory, each explaining the role of the sea, land and air forces in the operation with the help of a large map of the Normandy beaches and hinterland, sloped so that the audience could see it and the speaker could indicate the points he wished to bring to notice. "Great and sober confidence was evident throughout the meeting," Ramsay has recorded. Both he and Churchill emphasised the need for flexibility should events not go according to plan. Montgomery made it clear that he did not underestimate his chief opponent Rommel, for whose ingenuity and leadership he had a great respect. "We must blast our way on shore and get a good lodgement before the enemy can bring up sufficient reserves to turn us out," he declared. The proceedings closed with an address by the King who subsequently visited each of the assault forces in turn.

On May 25 all holders of the operation orders were directed to open them and three days later the Supreme Commander informed all concerned that D-day would be June 5. He also promulgated the H-hours for the various forces. From this moment all personnel became 'sealed' in their ships, all mail was impounded, telephone and cable facilities were forbidden and private telegrams allowed only in cases of emergency and with the permission of the Commanding Officer. On May 31 the intricate business of loading and assembly began and, to the credit of the planners, everything went smoothly. Enemy interference with this critical part of the operation was nil and by June 3 all was ready for the launching of the invasion.

SPECIAL MINELAYING OPERATIONS

May 28 saw the completion of Phase 3 of a special minelaying operation designed to give protection to the bombarding and assault forces from attacks by enemy 'E' and 'R' boats operating from Cherbourg and Le Havre. It was carried out by a force comprising the minelayers *Plover* and *Apollo,* four flotillas of motor launches and six flotillas of motor torpedo boats, assisted by aircraft of Bomber Command of the Royal Air Force. It involved the laying of 6,850 mines, of which about two-thirds were laid between the Dutch ports and Brest. A special type of mine was introduced during the operation designed to catch shallow draft craft and it was to prove most successful. During the last two phases, which continued right up to the eve of D-day, the laying of these mines was intensified, the surface ships concentrating on the ports of Le Havre, Cherbourg, Etretat, Calais, Boulogne and the Brittany coast, while aircraft covered Ijmuiden, the Hook of Holland, the West Scheldt, the Chenal du Four and Brest.

The completion of Exercise 'Fabius' marked the end of the training and exercise period for the assault forces. From now on all efforts were concentrated on ensuring that all ships and vessels would be ready to sail at the appointed time.

Laying on Sonic buoys

One of the final touches to the naval plan was made on May 31 when ten sonic underwater buoys were laid to mark the positions on the edge of the German minefield where the minesweepers would have to begin sweeping the channels decided upon. The buoys were inactive when laid but timed to come alive on D minus 1 day so that they could be located by the motor launches preceding the minesweepers, thus ensuring that sweeping began in the correct positions.

Final amendments

Admiral Ramsay had issued a warning that after 0900 on May 12 no further amendments to the plan would be allowed. This was designed to call a halt to the issue of amendments by assault force commanders which, unless checked, was liable to produce a critical situation so far as the recipients were concerned. However, on a higher plane, information received during the last few days of enemy troop concentrations in the Cotentin Peninsula necessitated a change in the plan for the airborne operations. In mid May an infantry division and a parachute regiment from Germany had taken up positions right on the dropping ground selected for the American paratroops. It was also learned that the 5th Parachute Division had moved to Rennes and it was rumoured the 17th Panzer Grenadiers were to move to Normandy from Poitiers. These last minute moves naturally raised doubts as to whether or not the enemy had discovered the Allied plan; in fact he had not and the moves were the result of Hitler's intuition that Normandy was the area most likely to be assaulted. However, they necessitated an alteration in the plan for the US airborne operations and a new route for the troop-carrying aircraft had to be chosen which would bring them close in proximity to the ships of Rear-Admiral Moon's Western Task Force. With some misgivings, Ramsay had imposed a total ban on A/A fire by ships of the Eastern Task Force for a similar reason and he now reluctantly extended it to those of Moon's force, but he warned the Air authorities that he could not guarantee its observance should an enemy air attack occur at the same time. His misgivings were unfortunately justified by the event.

THE WEATHER

As D-day approached the main pre-occupation of everyone at
Battle Headquarters from Eisenhower downwards was with the
weather. This was the one factor over which human control was
impossible and yet the whole success of the great enterprise
was dependent on it. In his book published in 1971 *Forecast for
Overlord*, Professor J. M. Stagg, CB, OBE, Chief Meteorological
adviser to the Supreme Commander, has described in great detail
the procedure employed for obtaining, recording and analysing the
meteorological information on which his forecasts of the weather
in the assault area were based. No stone was left unturned. The
weather maps of the Channel for the last fifty years were studied
in an attempt to discover a pattern for any given set of circumstances. Nature, however, is infinite in her variety and as Stagg has
recorded, "Even when the sequence of weather charts for one or
two days looked identical with the sequence in another year, the
immediately subsequent charts were almost invariably so dissim-
ilar as to be useless for prognostic purposes."[2] He had the difficult
task of reconciling the views of three groups of meteorologists, viz.
the American Widewing organisation, the Meteorological Office at
Dunstable and the Admiralty team in London. These were subsequently joined by the Staff Meteorological officers of the Naval
and Air Commanders-in-Chief, Ramsay and Leigh-Mallory. It is
not surprising that at these times there were differences of opinion
between these experts which were not easily resolved. Eisenhower
himself took a great personal interest in this part of his organisation and had instituted trial forecasts while he was still at his
headquarters in Bushy Park, so that as D-day approached, much
experience had been gained and he knew that he was certain to
receive the best possible advice from his meteorological adviser.

The crucial forecasting began with the move to Southwick Park
by the Supreme Commander and his staff during the week beginning May 29. Because of the complexity of the naval movements a
minimum forecast of 72 hours ahead was necessary, that is for
D-day and the two days following, and it was this last requirement
which produced so many headaches for the forecasters.

The library at Southwick House had been set apart for
Admiral Ramsay as his Mess. The walls were lined with

mahogany bookcases, now denuded of books, and it had been furnished with Admiralty pattern sofas and armchairs as well as a mahogany dining table and chairs. It was here that the important conferences on the launching of the invasion took place, over which Eisenhower presided and which were attended by the three Commanders-in-Chief and the Force Commanders with their Chiefs of Staff and other senior officers. The first conference took place on Monday, May 29, when Stagg forecast that while weather during the rest of the week would be operationally favourable, there was a risk of minor temporary disturbances at the weekend. This statement provoked enquiries regarding the duration and intensity of the disturbances to which, when pressed for his personal view, Stagg replied, "At this time of the year continuous spells of more than a few days of really stormy weather are infrequent. If the disturbed weather starts on Friday it is unlikely to last through both Monday (June 5 D-day) and Tuesday, but if it is delayed to Saturday and Sunday the weather on Monday and Tuesday could well be stormy."[3]

As the week wore on and conference succeeded conference, the prospects of favourable weather for D-day receded. On Friday, June 2, the Supreme Commander received the unwelcome information: "The whole situation from the British Isles to Newfoundland has been transformed in recent days and is now potentially full of menace."[4] This sombre statement produced a profound effect on all present and the tension was only relieved by a remark by Rear-Admiral Creasy, whose sense of humour never deserted him. As Stagg left the room he remarked, "There goes six feet two of Stagg and six foot one of gloom," at which everyone laughed. The following day, Saturday, June 3, was critical. It was essential for a decision to be taken whether or not to postpone the operation since some of the ships were already under way and proceeding towards the rendezvous south of the Isle of Wight, known as area 'Z'. It was a circle ten miles in diameter, the centre of which lay 14 miles southeast of St. Catherine's Lighthouse, and generally referred to as Piccadilly Circus.

At 2130 that evening everyone again filed into the conference room and settled down to hear what Stagg had to say. He confirmed the fears that he and his colleagues had expressed earlier about the weather for the next three or four days. Questions followed, particularly about the cloud and visibility which were of vital concern to the bombers and parachute troops. Eisenhower listened attentively to both questions and answers, then he posed a final one himself, "Were all the forecasting centres agreed on the forecast?" to which Stagg was thankful he could say, "Yes." Thereupon the Supreme Commander decided that the launching of the operation should be postponed on a day to day basis, but that a final decision would be taken at the next conference which would take place at 0415 the following morning. As the Admirals, Generals and Air Marshals emerged into the dimly lit hall, it was evident from their grave looks that they were extremely worried. Outside Southwick House the night was calm and clear, with no sign of the approaching bad weather that was threatening to wreck the carefully worked out plan for the assault on Normandy.

It was an anxious night of little sleep for the forecasters, who had to co-ordinate their views on the latest weather information at a telephone conference which began at 0300. Nothing, however, emerged to change their opinions and when, just over an hour later, Stagg re-entered the conference room the tension, he has recorded, was 'palpable'. After hearing what he had to say and consulting with his colleagues, Eisenhower confirmed that D-day would be postponed 24 hours to Tuesday, June 6.

EFFECT OF THE POSTPONEMENT

The postponement caused Ramsay considerable anxiety. The signal giving the decision was transmitted to all concerned at 0515/4 together with the revised H-hours consequent on the post-ponement. Convoys already at sea included Blockships from Oban and Bombarding ships from Belfast; these now were ordered to reverse course and proceed to sheltered anchorages. Only Group U.2A, a convoy of 138 vessels with four escorts and a rescue tug, destined for *Utah* beach, which had left ports in Devon on the evening of June 3 in accordance with its schedule, failed to receive the postponement signal. At 0900/4 it was 25 miles south of St. Catherine's Point and heading south. Two destroyers despatched from Plymouth at full speed failed to find it and ended up in a mine-field, of which more later, and it fell to a Walrus amphibian aircraft from Portsmouth to locate the convoy and persuade it to turn round and head up for Weymouth Bay. Owing, however, to the strong west-south-westerly wind now blowing and the short steep sea, the landing craft made slow progress and it was after midnight before the anchorage was reached. United States LCT 2498 broke down, capsized and sank off Portland, the crew fortunately being rescued.

About half an hour after Convoy U.2A had turned back, the 14th Minesweeping Flotilla which, in accordance with instructions, was sweeping the waters through which the "U" convoys would pass, discovered mines in a position 15 miles south of St. Catherine's Point, five of which were cut and two exploded in the sweep before worsening weather obliged the flotilla commander, Commander J. W. A. Irvine, RNVR, to abandon the operation. Convoy U.2A had a lucky escape and should not in fact have romped ahead of the minesweepers but the two destroyers, referred to above, landed up right in the middle of the swept mines and had to stop and wait until the minesweepers had disposed of them. When the information reached Ramsay he ordered a channel to be swept and buoyed through the area as soon as the weather moderated. In the event one of the unswept mines in this field which had been laid by an 'E' boat, claimed the first casualty in Operation Neptune, the minesweeper USS *Osprey*, which sank after striking it the following day, June 5.

THE SUBMARINE MARKERS

To the crews of the midget submarines X.20 (Lieutenant K.R. Hudspeth, RANVR, and X.23 (Lieutenant G.B. Honour, RNVR), to whom had been entrusted the highly important task of marking the limits of the British Assault area so as to eliminate any possibility of troops being landed in the wrong place, the receipt of the signal postponing the operation was anything but welcome. After a rough passage across the Channel in tow of the trawlers *Sapper* and *Dartheme* during June 2 they had been slipped at 0430/3 and, diving throughout the day, made their way at a depth of 30ft slowly towards the French coast. Every five hours they came to periscope depth, raised the induction pipe and started the engine to draw fresh air into the boat, a risky but necessary operation. They crossed the German minefield on the surface during the night of June 3/4 and reached their destinations about 0400/4. In X.23 the Deadreckoning position suggested that they were close to their final position so they lay on the bottom until 0800 and then rose gradually to periscope depth. They were off the mouth of the River Orne and the houses and buildings ashore were plainly visible. The position was fixed by cross-bearings of two churches and a hill, then they sank back to the bottom. The process was repeated at tea time, then they went back to the bottom until 2315. No message having been received, Honour now ran his craft inshore, using taut wire measuring gear, and anchored her in her marking position just before midnight. Then at 0100/5 the message postponing the operation was received and, as they were much too close inshore for comfort, he weighed and moved farther out to sea.

Crowded into the X craft's single cabin, measuring 5 feet and 8 inches by 5 feet, the crew of five, which included two additional officers from the Combined Operations Pilotage Party, now had to face sitting out the long day of June 5 submerged. They were too close to the enemy coast to risk surfacing to change the air which grew more and more foetid with each hour that passed. But stick it out they did, and not until 2315/5 did they surface, and then it was to receive the news that the Operation would take place the following day.

Their instructions were to remain on the bottom after reaching their assigned position, until twenty minutes before H-hour when they were to surface and switch on an automatic radio beacon and also a sonar set, the pulses of which could be picked up by the leading ships of the approaching convoys. Each submarine also carried an eighteen feet long telescopic mast, to which a small powerful flashing light showing to seaward was attached. If the light flashed green she was correctly on station, if red she was not. As an additional navigational aid each craft was to launch a rubber dinghy with an officer in it which, after drifting inshore a certain distance, was to anchor and exhibit a powerful light shining to seaward, to give the approaching landing craft some indication of her position relative to the beach itself. To ensure that the submarines were not run down by the onrushing assault craft they were to hoist a large yellow flag, which each Commanding Officer decided to supplement with a white Ensign.

The skill and endurance of these two submarine crews on which so much depended was to be commended by Admiral Ramsay who described their reports of proceedings as "masterpieces of understatement", as, with the modesty characteristic of men who volunteer for hazardous operations, no mention was made of the great hardships they had to endure.

The Momentous Decision

Back at Southwick House, on Sunday, June 4, the trees in the surrounding woods were beginning to sway under the influence of the rising wind while the sky filled with clouds, harbingers of the depression which Stagg and his colleagues had foretold. The day began badly with news of a hair-raising lapse of security. During the previous night an Associated Press teletype operator had decided to practise on an idle machine to improve her speeds. Almost without thinking she pressed the keys and typed out the message, "URGENT – PRESS ASSOCIATION NYK FLASH – EISENHOWER'S HEADQUARTERS ANNOUNCED ALLIED LANDINGS IN FRANCE." The machine was live and the dramatic message crossed the Atlantic. It was cancelled within thirty seconds but the damage, if any, had occurred. It was decided that all that could be done was to hope and pray that it had not reached the enemy. Post-war enquiries show that apparently it did not.

During the afternoon and evening of that fateful Sunday the forecasters pored over their charts, weighing every scrap of information reaching them from ships and shore stations to the westward. "No one could have imagined weather charts less propitious for the greatest military operation in history as those we had before us that Sunday evening," wrote Stagg. [5] But amidst the gloom, a ray of hope had started to gleam. When the Supreme Commander and the other senior officers assembled in the library at 2130 that night, Stagg was able to announce "some rapid and unexpected developments" had occurred over the North Atlantic and that it now looked as if conditions in the assault area on the morning of Tuesday, June 6, would meet the requirements laid down by the Sea and Air Commanders.

But the future outlook was less favourable. "Behind that fair interlude, cloud will probably increase again later on Tuesday . . . From early Wednesday until at least Friday, weather will continue unsettled." Here then was a dilemma. The Supreme Commander, as he says in his report, was "faced with the alternatives of taking the risks involved in an assault during what was likely to be only a partial and temporary break in the bad weather, or of putting off the operation for several weeks until tide and moon should again be favourable. Such a postponement, however, would have been most harmful to the morale of our troops, apart from the benefits of losing tactical surprise."[6] Moreover, once the assault took place, it was vital that the build-up should proceed unchecked and with great rapidity. That this was in everyone's mind was evident from the questions. In answer to Creasy's query whether conditions on Wednesday to Friday might be better than he had pictured them to be, Stagg replied, "There is a fair possibility that the depression we expect to bring a temporary deterioration later on Tuesday, may move in a more north-easterly direction than is assumed in the forecast. If that happens, both cloud and wind conditions will be more favourable than those I have given".[7] The Air Commanders were anxious about the cloud conditions. Eisenhower then asked Montgomery if he saw any reason why they should not go on Tuesday. His reply was "immediate and emphatic. 'I would say Go.'"[8] Some further discussion took place, particularly with regard to the effect on the estimated cloud conditions of the air operations, and, having heard everyone's views, the Supreme Commander made the momentous decision which he alone could make: the invasion would take place as planned on June 6. Ramsay and Montgomery were prepared to accept this decision as final, but Leigh-Mallory still had doubts and suggested that a further meeting be held the next morning to reconsider the matter.

For the forecasters, another sleepless night. At 0300 they held a telephone conference and Stagg was faced with the need to reconcile divergent views. He achieved unanimity only just in time for him to reach the conference room at 0415/5. "The atmosphere was sombre. Faces were grave and the room was quiet," as he entered. This time, however, he was the bearer of good news. The interval of fair weather on which the decision to launch the invasion was based would extend through all southern England during the night and would probably last into the late forenoon or afternoon of

Tuesday. Visibility would be good, wind force 3 mostly and not exceeding force 4 to 5 along the Normandy coast. Later on Tuesday, he expected cloud conditions to deteriorate and the forecast for the rest of the week was variable with considerable fair to fine periods.

"Immediately after I had finished speaking the tension seemed to evaporate and the Supreme Commander and his colleagues became as new men," says Stagg.[9] The die was now irrevocably cast and the whole vast machinery moved into top gear. That afternoon Rear-Admiral Sir Philip Vian, Commander of the Eastern Task Force, came to pay a final visit to the Commander-in-Chief. I accompanied him to the door as he left and we stood for a moment looking up at the overcast sky and listened to the wind sighing in the trees. "I don't know what you think," he said with a laugh, "but it certainly looks to me like bloody nonsense," and with that he got into his car and was driven away. Even Eisenhower felt obliged to seek confirmation of the improvement promised, so unfavourable did the conditions appear at Southwick Park. But Stagg and his colleagues were right; later that night, when I went out into the grounds for a final look round, I noticed that the clouds had broken and the wind had dropped. In the Operations room, soon after midnight, as the paratroops began to drop into the sleeping Normandy countryside, reports of improving conditions over the French coast also began to come in.

On the other side of the Channel the German meteorologists, with the limited information available to them, had decided that the weather was unsuitable for an Allied landing and, having the previous day notified von Rundstedt of his intentions, at 0700 on June 4 Rommel had left his headquarters at La Roche Guyon, halfway between Paris and the Normandy coast, for his home in Herrlingen. After attending a birthday party for his wife, he intended to visit Hitler at Obersalzburg and try to persuade him to send two more armoured divisions to Normandy, also an anti-craft corps and a brigade armed with the new V weapons. Admiral Krancke, Commander Naval Group West, having informed von Rundstedt that the weather was too rough for the patrol craft at Cherbourg and Brest to leave harbour, had himself left Bordeaux on an inspection tour. As mentioned in Chapter 2, German intelligence had warned all military commanders in the West of the interception of a message alerting the French Resistance to the imminence of an invasion, but only the XVth Army Group had reacted to this information. As Admiral Ruge remarks, "On the morning of June 5, 1944, there was nothing to indicate that the decision to launch an attack had been taken on the other side of the Channel and that a gigantic armada was getting under way preparatory to commencing an assault on Fortress Europe."[10] In fact the senior commanders of the VIIth Army Group had been ordered to assemble at Rennes in Brittany for a map exercise arranged for the forenoon of June 6. Although instructed not to leave their commands before dawn on that day, several had in fact done so. General Speidel took the opportunity of his Chief's absence to invite a few friends to dinner that Monday night. "The conversation was very lively; it covered such matters as Italy, Russia, French politics, the French Navy, Hitler's lack of information, the situation in the United States and many other subjects."[11] By midnight all the guests had departed, but Speidel and some of the staff sat up talking. At 0135 the telephone rang: "Paratroops landing on the east coast of the Cotentin Peninsula" – the unsuspected invasion had begun.

Notes

1 Samuel Morison, *History of US Naval Operations in World War II,* Vol XI.
2 J.M. Stagg, *Forecast for Overlord.*
3 Ibid.
4 Ibid.
5 Ibid.
6 Supreme Commander's Report.
7 Stagg, ibid.
8 Stagg, ibid.
9 Stagg, ibid.
10 Friedrich Ruge, *Rommel Face au Débarquement 1944.*
11 Ibid.

Chapter Five

The Assault

At noon on June 1, 1944 Admiral Ramsay assumed operational command of all the forces allocated to Operation Neptune and from then on he was in general control of all operations in the Channel. On June 4 the First Sea Lord, Admiral of the Fleet Sir Andrew B. Cunningham, visited him at Southwick House. They were old friends and at this critical moment he wanted to assure him of his full support and confidence in the great operation about to commence. On the afternoon of the same day Ramsay issued a special Order of the Day to the officers and men of the Allied navies and the merchantmen under his command. It read:

> "It is our privilege to take part in the greatest amphibious operation in history – a necessary preliminary to the opening of the Western front in Europe which, in conjunction with the great Russian advance, will crush the fighting power of Germany.
>
> This is the opportunity which we have long awaited and which must be seized and pursued with relentless determination: the hopes and prayers of the free world and of the enslaved peoples of Europe will be with us and we cannot fail them.
>
> Our task, in conjunction with the Merchant Navies of the United Nations, and supported by the Allied Air Forces, is to carry the Allied Expeditionary Force to the Continent, to establish it there in a secure bridgehead and to build it up and maintain it at a rate which will outmatch that of the enemy.

Let no one underestimate the magnitude of this task.

The Germans are desperate and will resist fiercely until we out-manoeuvre and out-fight them which we can and will do. To every one of you will be given the opportunity to show by his determination and resource that dauntless spirit of resolution which individually strengthens and inspires and which collectively is irresistible.

I count on every man to do his utmost to ensure the success of this great enterprise which is the climax of the European war.

Good luck to you all and Godspeed."

(Sgd) B.H. RAMSAY, Admiral
Allied Naval Commander-in-Chief
Expeditionary Force

DEPARTURE

During the early forenoon of June 5 the assault and support forces berthed at ports in the south of England started to get under way, and head out into the Channel. An umbrella of fighter aircraft droned overhead ready to pounce on any enemy reconnaissance aircraft which might put in an appearance, but none was in evidence. From the crowded anchorage of Spithead the sailing proceeded smoothly, a steady stream of ships passing the Nab Tower to the east and the Needles to the west and heading for Piccadilly Circus. The wind was west force 5 easing to force 3 to 4 during the day and veering to west-north-west as the day wore on. These were severe conditions for the smaller landing craft but, as the Naval Commander Eastern Task Force, Rear-Admiral Sir Philip Vian, was to write of them, "Their spirit and seamanship alike rose to meet the greatness of this hour and they pressed forward . . . in high heart and resolution; there was no faltering."[1] For the Assault Group S2, based on Newhaven, the 33 miles beat up to windward into a head sea made it difficult to keep up to schedule and ships leaving the Needles Channel met a strong flood stream which, together with the wind, made it extremely difficult to weather the western end of the Isle of Wight.

Admiral Vian, in his flagship the cruiser HMS *Scylla*, left Spithead at 1630 so as to join the assault groups in area 'Z' before dark. Once these had altered to a southerly course conditions for the larger ships were easier, but smaller ones had great difficulty in steering with a beam wind and sea and of keeping within the limits of the swept channels.

Admiral Alan G. Kirk, Naval Commander of the Western Task Force, in his flagship the cruiser USS *Augusta*, sailed from Portland at midday to overtake Assault Groups 'O' and 'U' and Follow-up Force 'B' as they reached area 'Z'. Group U2A which, as has been related, had only reached Weymouth Bay in the small hours of that morning, had made heroic efforts to repair weather damage and to refuel and, to the lasting credit of the officers and men concerned, when all too soon the time came to get under way again, 128 LCTs out of 135 were ready for sea.

Joining the Assault Groups as they entered the swept channels and providing welcome evidence of the might of Allied sea-power, came the battleships, cruisers and destroyers of the bombarding forces, while out on the flanks, A/S vessels and aircraft kept watch for any U-boats which might attempt to impede their progress. In the event the absence of enemy reaction was so noticeable that Admiral Vian was prompted to remark in his report, "It may probably be that weather conditions had some part in what must ever be a matter for wonder, that the embarkation, sailing and passage of the force by day should have been carried through without so great a movement being detected by a well equipped, prepared and determined enemy. That this should have been achieved is a lasting tribute to the admirable work of the Allied Air Force and the excellence of the cover plan."

MINESWEEPING OPERATIONS

Leading the Assault force towards its objective were some of its smallest ships. These were the Harbour Defence Motor Launches (HDMLs) fitted with minesweeping gear which preceded the leading ship of each minesweeping flotilla to minimise the chance of her striking a mine. Although their inclusion entailed some loss of speed and cutting power by the fleet sweepers they were to prove their worth.

From area 'Z' five swept channels had been selected leading south-south-eastward. Just before entering the German minefield guarding the French coast each channel split into two, one for the fast (12 knot) and one for the slow (5 knot) convoys. These ten channels were numbered consecutively from west to east. All during that Monday afternoon the ten flotillas of fleet minesweepers ploughed steadily southwards towards the Normandy coast. Following close behind came the 42 dan-laying trawlers marking the swept channels with lighted dan buoys. Before entering the minefield proper, five more mines were discovered in the field previously located by the 14th Minesweeping flotilla and, as already mentioned, a sixth caused the loss of USS *Osprey* of the 7th US Minesweeping squadron, but within the German mined area the results were far less than expected. However, as might be surmised, experiences varied. The 1st flotilla, sweeping channel number 9 ahead of Force 'S', found no mines at all, the 9th flotilla preceding Force 'J', the 14th, Force 'U' and the 18th, Force 'G' all cut mines. In channels 2, 6 and 7 a total of 29 mines were swept. The tidal stream proved stronger than expected and some ships were obliged to steer as much as 20 degrees off the course it was desired to make good in order to keep in the channel.

The 14th flotilla, sweeping channel 2, was the first to sight the French coast which was plainly in view at 1940. With nearly three hours of daylight still to go, and with memories of Greece and Crete in their minds, the total lack of enemy reaction was quite inexplicable to the crews as they stood by their anti-aircraft guns. The 16th flotilla, sweeping channel 1, sighted the coast an hour later and closed to within eleven miles, but still there was no enemy reaction. Post-war enquiries have failed to explain the reason for this lack of vigilance on the enemy's part, which may have been due to the light and also to the fact, as related later, that the Allied Air Forces had taken a heavy toll of his radar installations, while those remaining in action were being jammed.

During the sweeping of the channels the positions of the minesweepers were checked by radar and also by taut wire measuring gear, and it is a tribute to the navigational skill of these small ships that all the flotillas laid the terminal buoys of their swept channels within one cable (200 yards) of the planned position and within a few minutes of the time laid down in the plan.

However, the minesweepers' task was not finished when they reached the southern end of the ten swept channels. Their next task was to sweep an area parallel to the beaches in which landing ships and transports could anchor safely and unload their troops, stores and equipment. They also had to sweep the area allotted to the bombarding ships. It was not an easy matter for them to adjust their movements to their new tasks without getting in each other's way and they became more concerned at dodging each other than with possible interference by enemy shore batteries under the muzzles of the silent guns of which they were manoeuvring.

On the completion of the off-shore sweeping programme the minesweepers' next task was to widen the ten channels so as to form one broad one across the mined area, which became known as the 'Spout'. Before D-day drew to a close they would have swept the spaces between channels 3 and 4, and 5 and 6. The success of the minesweeping operation was indeed remarkable and made an outstanding contribution to that of the whole under-taking. Admiral Ruge is very critical of the failure of Marine Goup West to reinforce the mine barrier with new mines and to lay ground mines with all kinds of delay action fuses off the beaches, all of which would have made the task of the Allied minesweepers much more difficult than it was. [2]

THE AIRBORNE ASSAULT

While the minesweepers were busy off the Normandy coast with the second of their operations, and the leading ships of the assault groups were advancing down the channels they had swept, "Almost on the stroke of midnight the whole coast in front of us awoke to a frenzy of brilliant white flashes and thunderous deto-nations," wrote Lieutenant (S) William H. Pugsley, RCNVR, serving on board a 'Bangor' class minesweeper of the 31st Canadian manned flotilla.[3] This was the beginning of the air bombardment of the beach area and surrounding defences, aimed at softening them up and preventing the enemy from detecting the approach of the assault forces. It also served to distract his atten-tion from the arrival of the Pathfinder aircraft and the three airborne divisions of British and United States troops due to begin dropping in specially selected areas behind the beaches at 0130/6. These troops had very important tasks to perform which included the seizure of certain bridges before they could be blown up and the destruction of others by which the enemy might otherwise have rushed reinforcements to the area. Although everything did not go exactly according to plan, the main objectives were achieved and the enemy was taken completely by surprise.

RADAR COUNTERMEASURES AND ENEMY REACTIONS

The Germans had constructed a chain of radar stations covering the entire coastline of western Europe. In North-western France a major coastal station had been erected every ten miles and these were backed by other stations farther inland. The whole formed part of the Luftwaffe's defence system against the increasing weight of Allied air attack. In addition the German Navy had built a number of radar stations with a range of 25 to 30 miles for the detection of shipping, and much reliance was placed upon them. During the week before D-day , however, ten of these were systematically and accurately attacked by the Royal Air Force and during the night of June 5/6 all but a few of the remaining radar stations were jammed, care being taken to leave enough sets operating north of the Seine to make sure that the Germans would detect the bogus convoys which were to be simulated by twelve Motor Launches equipped with barrage balloons. Eight of these manoeuvred on a 14 mile front to seaward of Cap d'Antifer, the flank ships reaching positions off Bruneval and Fecamp about 0430/6. To the westward the remaining four craft, operating under the naval commander Force 'U', manoeuvred six miles to the east of Cap Barfleur (the light on which was burning brightly as in peace time) between 0230 and 0440. Assisting in this deception were some 100 aircraft which flew round and round dropping bundles of tinfoil know as 'window' and adjusting their movements so as gradually to draw nearer and nearer to the coast in the manner of an approaching convoy. The same procedure was adopted off Boulogne. The results exceeded all expectations. Between 0100 and 0400 whilst the assault convoys were approaching the beaches, out of 92 radar stations only nine were in operation; the airborne assault aircraft were not intercepted, the Luftwaffe having sent its available fighters on a wild goose chase over Rennes, and the invasion fleet was not detected until Force 'U' arrived off *Utah* beach at 0230/6.

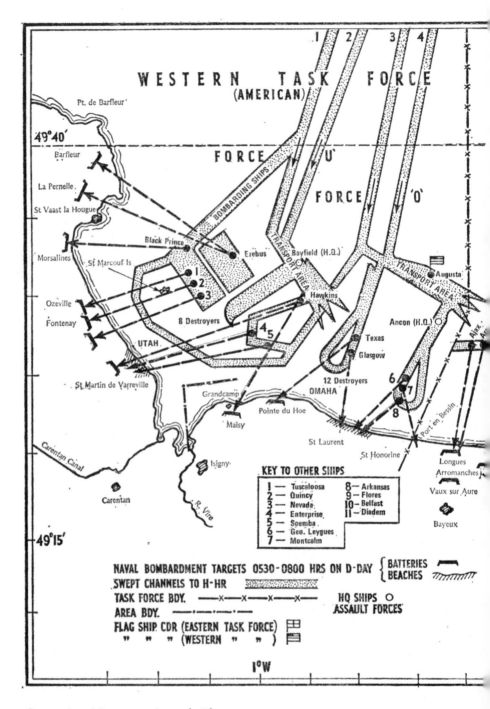

Operation Neptune: Assault Phase.

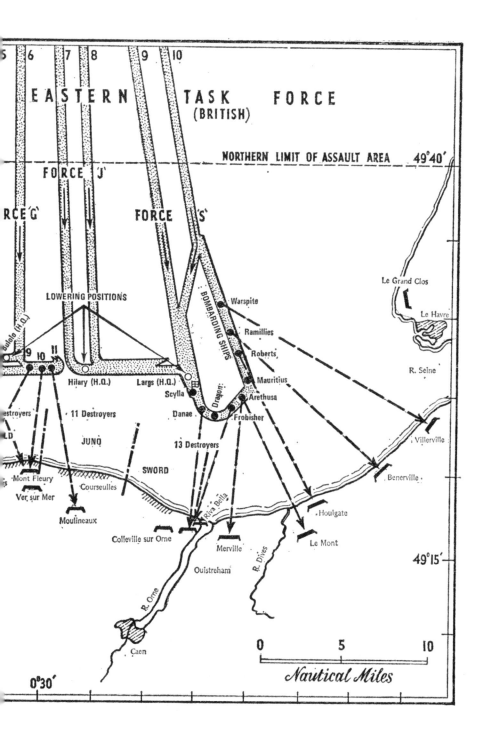

5 6 7 8 9 10

EASTERN TASK FORCE
(BRITISH)

NORTHERN LIMIT OF ASSAULT AREA   49°40'

FORCE 'J'

RCE 'G'   FORCE 'S'

Le Grand Clos

Le Havre

LOWERING POSITIONS

BOMBARDING SHIPS

Warspite

ulolo (H.Q.)

Ramillies

9 10 11

Roberts

R. Seine

Hilary (H.Q.)   Largs (H.Q.)   Mauritius

estroyers   Scylla

LD   11 Destroyers   Danae   Arethusa

Frobisher

JUNO   Villerville

13 Destroyers

SWORD   Benerville

Mont Fleury

Courseulles

Ver sur Mer   Riva Bella   Houlgate

Moulineaux   Le Mont

Colleville sur Orne

Merville   R. Dives

Ouistreham

R. Orne   49°15'

Caen   0   5   10

0°30'   *Nautical Miles*

Thanks also to the dummy parachutists fitted with fire-crackers to simulate small arms fire, dropped over a wide area, it was a long time before von Rundstedt's headquarters were able to form any clear idea of the situation. Not until 0309 did Naval Group West order 'E' boats and patrol craft to sea to patrol the Baie de la Seine and, in response to the Motor Launches deception, the coast between Dieppe and le Treport. The uncertainty persisted throughout the night as is revealed by an entry in the Operations Log of Naval Group West for 0500/6: "Supreme Command, West – and apparently also Army Group 'B' – are uncertain what countermeasures to order as they do not know whether the enemy landing up to this time is a dummy landing, a diversionary manoeuvre, or the main landing."[4]

THE ASSAULT

"Gentlemen, what Philip of Spain failed to do, what Napoleon tried and failed to do and what Hitler never had the courage to try, we are about to do and, with God's grace we shall." With those words Rear-Admiral Creasy had concluded his briefing of the war correspondents assembled to witness and report on the greatest amphibious operation ever attempted. That expectation was now about to be fulfilled, as the five assault convoys neared the positions off the beaches on which they were to land. Since, as has been mentioned, the earliest H-hours were those at *Utah* and *Omaha* the landings will be described as they occurred working from west to east.

UTAH BEACH

H-hour for the landing on *Utah* beach was 0630 and exactly on schedule at 0229 Rear-Admiral D. P. Moon, USN, Commanding Naval Force 'U' in his flagship USS *Bayfield*, reached the transport area 11½ miles east of *Utah* beach and came to anchor in 17 fathoms. In company were the 116 ships of Force U2A (1) carrying the first wave of the assault troops and the bombardment squadron comprising the battleships USS *Tuscaloosa* and *Quincy* with HMS *Hawkins, Enterprise* and *Black Prince,* HMNS *Soemba* and eight US destroyers. *(See Appendix IV.)* The follow-up Group U2A(2) of

127 ships, which had suffered so severely from its false start was scheduled to reach the transport area at 0330.

The passage had proved uneventful, the 'E' boats ordered out of Cherbourg having been obliged to return to base on account of the weather. The transport area had been swept for mines and the 34 minesweepers (16 US and 18 British) were still busy completing the sweeping of the approach lanes and fire support areas. Unfortunately in this sector the Germans had laid mines with delay action fuses, which only became active after they had been swept several times and these, supported by mines dropped by aircraft, were to be responsible for most of the casualties incurred in this sector.

While the transports are unloading their troops into the personnel carriers (LCVP) let us take a quick look at the coast they are about to assault.

The nine mile stretch of the east coast of the Cotentin Peninsula, between the villages of St. Martin de Varreville and La Madeleine which had been selected for the landing, is low-lying and featureless. The gently sloping beach of yellow sand had been obstructed by several lines of obstacles to a total depth of 300 to 400 yards at low water. Above high water mark lay a belt of sand dunes 100 to 200 yards wide against which, on the seaward side, the Germans had built a low concrete wall. Behind the beach the pasture land had been flooded, but it was crossed by causeways to which exits in the dunes gave access. The enemy had installed 28 fixed and mobile batteries comprising 111 guns along the coast and inland from it, of which eight were casemated and most of them were capable of firing onto the beach. Four miles off shore lay two small islands named St. Marcouf, on which it was suspected the enemy might have guns and/or radar. In the event the 132 US Rangers sent to capture them found them deserted but mined and booby trapped. Running southeastward from the islands was a shoal called Cardonnet Bank on which the enemy had sown ground mines and which was crossed by the boat channels leading from the transport area to the beaches. These mines proved troublesome and caused several casualties. On account of the long run-in from the transport area to the shore, two Patrol Craft had been detailed as navigational aids, one for each half of the beach, designated Green Tare and Red Uncle. They were assisted by four Landing Craft Control (LCC).

69

At 0430 the first wave of assault troops set out from the transports on their two hour voyage to the shore. Until they reached the lee of the land they had a very unpleasant time bucking into a head wind and sea; as a result most of the troops were seasick. It was intended that eight LCTs, each carrying four DD Tanks, should accompany the first wave of troops but they were delayed by weather and did not reach the transport area until 0445, half an hour after they should have left it. The control officer in PC1176, appreciating that the tanks would be too late if launched two and a half miles off shore as intended, led the convoy to within a mile of the shore where the water was relatively calm, before launching them so that they reached the beach only ten minutes late. However, one control boat and one LCT were lost when they were mined crossing the Cordonnet Bank.

Dawn broke bright and clear over the Cotentin Peninsula giving the German gunners the advantage of the light with the invading forces silhouetted against the eastern horizon. At 0505 a battery opened fire on the destroyers USS *Fitch* and *Corry* who had taken up their bombarding positions 3 and 2½ miles respectively off the coast on the northern flank of the landing area. At 0520 276 bombers of the IXth US Army Air Force came in below the clouds and blasted the batteries with 4,400 bombs without, however, completely silencing them, for twenty minutes later a heavy battery in the St. Vaast-la-Hogue area took some of the minesweepers under fire and was promptly engaged by HMS *Black Prince*, who drew the fire on herself. The scheduled time for the bombardment to begin was 0550 but the enemy, having jumped the gun, Admiral Morton L. Deyo, USN, in command of the bombarding squadron, gave the order to 'Open Fire' at 0536. From then on, for the next three-quarters of an hour, all hell broke loose as the 14in guns of the *Nevada* and the 15in ones of the *Erebus*, supported by the smaller guns of the cruisers and destroyers, pounded the enemy defences. Air spotting was provided by aircraft of the Royal Air Force and Fleet Air Arm operating from shore bases in Britain, and some of the pilots were seconded from the US Navy. At 0610 aircraft started to lay a smoke screen between the shore and the ships to shield the approaching landing craft, but a gap in the screen resulting from the shooting down of one aircraft exposed the destroyer *Corry* and she became the target of several batteries. In endeavouring to manoeuvre in the restricted waters to spoil the enemy's aim, she struck a mine which broke her back and at 0641 she began to settle and was abandoned.

Right on schedule the first wave of the assault troops was approaching the shore and when it was some 700 yards short the 4.7in guns of the LCGs of the support force on either flank began to plaster the defences from close range, and just before the troops touched down, 17 Landing Craft Tank (Rocket) (LCT (R)) let fly their deadly salvoes. The effect of all this detonation was to raise a cloud of dust and smoke which completely obscured the shore and a strong tidal stream carried the landing craft some 1,500 yards south of the beaches on which they were scheduled to land. As it happened this was a fortunate turn of events, since at the beach where they landed almost no opposition was encountered and the beach obstacles had not been armed with explosives and booby traps, whereas farther north the defences were stronger and more heavily manned. The first wave touched down at 0635, only five minutes late, and after a short period of initial bewilderment as to their location the troops made rapid progress inland, so that by 0745 the village of St. Martin de Varreville was in American hands. In all 26 assault waves, excluding the DD tanks, followed one another at intervals of between ten and twenty minutes, though there was a pause between waves 5 and 6 due to a false report that Green beach was being heavily shelled. By 0945 fifteen waves had landed successfully. The naval demolition teams and army engineers who had landed with the second wave, soon had wide sections of the beaches clear of obstacles, though they had suffered some casualties as enemy artillery, mortar and machine guns began to register on the beaches. These were immediately engaged by the bombarding and support ships and the effectiveness of naval gunfire was plainly demonstrated. Admiral Moon remarked in his report: "The neutralisation of these formidable batteries by the bombardment group was so effective that these batteries offered little opposition to either the assault or follow up."[5]

In addition to the losses already mentioned, the only other ones were three LCTs and one LCF, all believed to have been mined.

The General commanding the US 4th Division, Major-General Barton and his staff, landed at 1400 and set up his headquarters ashore and by 1800, 21,328 troops, 1,742 vehicles and 1,695 tons of stores had been landed on *Utah* beach.

The landing at *Utah* in fact went according to plan and in sharp contrast to that at *Omaha*.

OMAHA BEACH

The landing at *Omaha* was to prove the most difficult and costly of all the five assaults on the Normandy coast; as a result it is generally referred to as 'Bloody' *Omaha*. Faulty intelligence, which suggested that this section of the coast was lightly held by a German conscript division, whereas in mid March the western sector had been taken over by the battle-tried 352nd Division, and the fact that the defences were much tougher than suspected, both contributed to the near disaster which overtook the forces which landed on the eastern sector; but, as will be seen, there were other reasons.

From the estuary of the river Vire, at the base of the Cotentin Peninsula eastward to Port en Bessin, the character of the coast changes. Instead of sloping gently down to the sea it rises abruptly to produce a line of high precipitous cliffs fronted by wide sandy beaches, to which access can only be obtained through narrow, easily fortifiable ravines. The section selected for the assault was a three and a half mile stretch to the eastward of a point four miles east of the Pointe du Hoc; at either end of this curving beach the cliffs were 100 feet high, but in the middle it sloped upwards to a plateau 150 feet high half a mile inshore. There were four gaps in this escarpment which had been cut by watercourses and these provided the only possible exits. The beach itself, like that at *Utah*, was of firm sand but the inshore end was marked by a bank of shingle which rose sharply. Along the western third of the beach a concrete sea wall had been built, but elsewhere the shingle gave way to sand dunes backed by coarse tufted grass. The only paved road in the area was running along the coast west from the village of Les Moulins to Vierville, where it turned inland. The Germans had made good use of the natural features in planning their defences. The tidal sector of the beach had been well planted with obstructions armed with explosives. Above the shingle bank were barbed wire entanglements and mines, and all the exits were blocked with mines and/or concrete obstructions and anti-tank ditches. Covering the beach were sixteen strong points comprising bunkers and pill-boxes equipped with light artillery, anti-tank guns and machine guns. Fire positions, invisible from seaward, had been built into the cliffs at either end and were capable of taking the beach under flank fire from both directions.

Although the Allies suspected that it would be a fairly tough nut to crack, this was the only section of beach between the Vire and Port en Bessin considered suitable on which to land.

As had been mentioned, all beaches in the Neptune plan had been divided alphabetically into sectors to which phonetic code names were attached, those at *Omaha* being designated Able to George. The actual assault beaches were designated Dog, Easy and Fox and these were further subdivided into sections *Dog* – Green, White and Red, *Easy* – Green and Red, and *Fox* – Green.

Force 'O', under its commander, Rear-Admiral John L. Hall, USN, approached without incident down swept channels 3 and 4. In the van was the Bombarding Squadron, Force 'C', under Rear-Admiral C.F. Bryant, USN, with his flag in the battleships USS *Texas* and in company with the oldest battleships in the US Navy, USS *Arkansas,* the cruisers HMS *Glasgow,* FFS *George Leygues* (flagship Rear-Admiral Jaujard) and *Montcalm* and seven US destroyers. Following Force 'C' came Group O1 comprising the flagship USS *Ancon,* fifteen transports, 33 LCIs (L), 2 LCH escorted by two US and three British destroyers. Bringing up the rear was the slow convoy O2 comprising 267 landing ships and miscellaneous craft.

The bombarding ships proceeded to their assigned stations east and west of the assault area and anchored at about 0220/6. Half an hour later Group O1 anchored in the transport area which, like that at *Utah,* was eleven miles off shore, a distance determined by the supposed threat presented by the enemy's shore batteries. However, lacking the protection of the Cotentin Peninsula, conditions for lowering and manning the assault craft were extremely rugged in this exposed anchorage, the wind being south-west force 5, the sea very choppy, the sky partly overcast and visibility about ten miles.

The pre-landing bombardment by Force 'C', due to begin at 0550, was anticipated by an enemy battery near Port en Bessin opening

	FORMATIONS OF LCA		HEADQUARTERS SHIP		MAJOR SUPPORT CRAFT
	LC INFANTRY	LS INFANTRY	LC TANKS/VEHICLES		LC HQ^S & ML^S

GROUP		COMPOSITION OF GRP	LEAVE LP	TOUCH DOWN
1	ML — LCH LOWERING POSITION	2 LC (NAV^N) 1 LC (HQ) 1 ML 8 LCT DD TANKS 3 LCS (L) 3 LCG (L) 8 LCP (L)	H - 125	H - 7½
2	10 LCA — 10 LCA	1 LCH 10 LCT (AVRE) 20 LCA ASSAULT COY.^{S} 2 LCF 9 LCA (HR) 8 LCT (A) 1 LCT (CB)	H - 90	H HOUR
3		5 LCT (R)	H - 76	
4	GRP 4A 33RD FD REG^T GP4 76TH. FD REG^T GP 4B 7TH FD REG^T	18 LCT (SP) 3 ML^S	H - 65	GP 4 H + 75 GP 4A H + 105 GP 4B H + 195
5	22 LCA 18 LCA	2 LCF 40 LCA RES ASS. COY.^{S} LCO CU BE	H — 60	H + 20
6	8 LCA 6 LCA 8 LCA	2 LCI (L) 14 LCA (COMMANDOS) 8 LCA (TOWED) RE	H - 50	H + 30
7		9 LCT (PRIORITY VEHICLES) 3 LCT (WADING TANKS)	H - 40	H + 45
8	18 LCA	3 LCI (L) 18 LCA (RESERVE BN)	H - 20	.H + 60
9		12 LCI (S) COMMANDOS	H + 35	H + 75
9A		10 LCI (S) COMMANDOS	H + 65	H + 105
10		9 LCT (2ND PRIORITY VEHICLES) 2 LCT STORES	H + 35	H + 120

Typical Deployment of an assault brigade at the lowering position.

fire on the *Arkansas* at 0530, to which she replied. It was a tense moment for the two Free French ships when ordered to open fire on their homeland but, as Admiral Jaujard remarked to American historian Rear-Admiral Morison, "It was part of the price we had to pay for defeat in 1940." At 0600 an aerial bombardment of the beach defences was due to take place, but because of the low cloud and fear of hitting their own troops, a 30 second delay had been imposed on the bombers with the result that the bombs fell three miles inland and the only victims were some cattle and pigs.

Meanwhile the assault forces had been making their rough and uncomfortable way to the departure line two miles off shore, where they were marshalled by Control craft. The intended order of landing of the first four waves on all beaches was:

H-10 to H-5 minutes – DD tanks
H-hour – LCT (A) scarrying tanks and armoured bulldozers for beach clearance
H + 1 minute – Infantry
H + 3 minutes – Demolition parties

The plan was to launch the DD tanks three miles off shore unless the weather conditions made this inadvisable, the decision resting jointly with the senior naval officer in the LCTs and the senior army tank officer in each assault group. The DD tanks in Group O1 were launched two and a half miles from the beach and all but five sank in the choppy sea, three of the survivors owing their escape to the initiative of Ensign H. P. Sullivan, USNR, in command of LCT 600 who, seeing his first tank founder, pulled up his ramp and drove inshore to land the remaining three on the beach. On the right flank it was decided that conditions were too bad for launching and the LCTs carrying the DD tanks, after having paused to allow the LCT (A)s carrying more tanks to catch up, disembarked on the beach at 0629 with their guns blazing.

The bombarding ships, aided by the flank support groups, continued to pound the defences until five minutes before H-hour, but the failure of the air bombing meant that the former had insufficient time to neutralise the defences before the tanks and troops landed, with disastrous results. The first wave of assault troops touched down on beaches Dog, Easy and Fox at about 0635 and were met with intense machine gun and mortar fire. In many cases the troops had to wade 50 to 100 yards through the obstacles covering 200 to 300 yards of beach before they could hope to reach the protection of the sea wall or the shingle bank. Few succeeded in making it. The demolition parties, too, lost much of their equipment in the surf and the rapidly rising tide soon put them out of business and they too suffered many casualties. Nevertheless they succeeded in clearing five of the sixteen lanes planned.

The strong east-going tidal stream swept some of the control boats out of position and troops were landed farther along the coast than intended and this added to the confusion. "All along *Omaha* there was a disunited, confused and partly leaderless body of infantry, without cohesion, with no artillery support, huddled under the sea wall to get shelter from the withering fire. There were long stretches of beach where no one had landed. Only two companies out of eight were on the beaches where they were supposed to be."[6]

When the second wave landed at 0700 there was no sign of slackening in the enemy's resistance and an hour later in the western sector neither a man nor a vehicle had succeeded in leaving the beaches. Things looked grim, but the situation was saved by the initiative of the destroyer commanders who took their ships into within 800 yards of the shore and despite, in many cases, the absence of shore fire control parties, blasted every target of opportunity with their guns. In this they were ably supported by the support groups and gradually they got the better of the defenders. At 1030 the troops of the follow-up Group O2 were landed and thus all the assault troops of Force 'O' were now committed to the attack. It is in adversity that men so often show their finest qualities. Slowly, steadily and with great courage, the men of the US First Division fought their way inland and the tables were turned on the defenders as tanks managed to get into action and the strong points were silenced. At one time the responsible Generals were fearful that the attack might falter, but Rear-Admiral Hall who, as we have seen, was responsible for the landing until the troops were firmly established ashore, reassured them that, "there was such power behind the assault it could not fail." The turning point came about 1100 and by 1340 beaches Dog and Easy were clear of opposition except for desultory artillery and mortar fire, which was still deadly accurate.

Meanwhile, much effort was being expended on the destruction of a supposed powerful battery sited at Pointe du Hoc, three and a half miles west of Dog beach. It had been heavily shelled before H-hour by the battleship *Texas* and so far had not betrayed its presence by firing a shot. Due to a navigational error the three companies of Rangers detailed to capture and silence it did not land until 0705, by which time the Germans in the surrounding strong points had recovered and remanned their positions. The Rangers were fully equipped to scale the 100 feet high cliffs out of which great lumps had been torn by the *Texas'* fourteen inch shells, and they were now supported by the destroyers HMS *Tallybont* and USS *Satterlee,* but they did not reach the top without suffering many casualties from the German defenders who fought back tenaciously. When they eventually did so they discovered that although the gun mountings were there, the guns themselves had been replaced by telegraph poles whilst the work of constructing a casemate was proceeding. However, the Rangers fought their way through to the road running between Vierville and Grandcamp, where they established a defensive position which they held for two days until relieved.

About 1430 the Reserve Group Assault Force 'B', in 48 LSTs under Commodore C. D. Edgar, USN, stood into the assault area and anchored close to the beaches and at 1715 the Commanding General 1st Division, Major-General C. J. Huebner, and his staff left USS *Ancon* and set up his headquarters ashore. By now the work of organising the beaches for further unloading was proceeding in an orderly manner, the beachhead was established, the problem now was to build it up.

It is in the nature of things that there should have been much criticism of the conduct of the landing at *Omaha* in view of the heavy casualties suffered. No exact figure for these is available but reliable information suggests that they were in the region of 4,000. Although, as we have seen, mistakes were made, the enduring memory of the landing is the way in which the officers in command of the destroyers, support and landing craft rose to the occasion and how the troops of the 1st US Division, after an initial setback, rallied and fought their way to ultimate victory.

GOLD BEACH

The three British-Canadian beaches were sited along a 25 mile stretch of the coast between Port en Bessin and the mouth of the River Orne, the westernmost one of the three being named *Gold*. Like *Utah* and *Omaha*, the beaches were subdivided into sectors, those on *Gold* beach designated How, Item, Jig and King. It was planned in the first instance to land on sectors Jig and King while a separate force would capture Port en Bessin. The coast along the assault beaches was low-lying, the high cliffs which extended four miles east of Port en Bessin giving way to sandy bluffs not more than 50 feet high. There were no extensive inundations but the enemy had constructed a number of strong points capable of enfilading the beaches, though not of firing to seaward, so confident was he that any landing would be made at High Water. The most formidable battery in the area was one of four 6in guns sited at Longues and overlooking the How sector. Farther east behind Item sector were one 3.4in and two 2.9in guns and directly opposite King sector was a casemated battery of four 4.5in guns.

Force 'G', commanded by Commodore C. E. Douglas-Pennant with his broad pennant in the headquarters ship HMS *Bulolo*, reached the lowering position 6.7 miles off the beaches without incident via channels 5 and 6 at 0455/6. Preceding the force was the Bombarding Force 'K', comprising the cruisers HMS *Orion*, *Ajax*, *Argonaut* and *Emerald* with HMNS *Flores* and fourteen destroyers. The Support Force was composed of three Landing Craft Gun (Large), eight Landing Craft Tank (Rocket), four Landing Craft Support (Large), seven Landing Craft Flak and three regiments of SP Artillery in sixteen Landing Craft Tank (Armoured), and was included amongst the three Groups which made up Force 'G', totalling 243 ships.

H-hour for Force 'G' was 0725 and it was preceded by a sustained bombardment of the enemy defences beginning at 0545. This, lasting longer than had been possible at *Utah* and *Omaha* beaches, was effective in silencing the batteries referred to above except the one at Longues, which had also been bombed during the night but had survived because of its concrete casemate. However, when at 0557 it opened fire on HMS *Bulolo*, which in consequence was obliged to shift berth, it

78

Top Left: HMS *Stornoway* – a Bangor class minesweeper, one of the 89 used to clear the approaches to the Normandy Beaches. /IWM

Left: A British Yard Minesweeper designed for inshore minesweeping, a large number of which were employed keeping the assault area clear of mines. /IWM

Above: HMS *Hilary*, Headquarters ship of Commodore 1st Class G. N. Oliver, Commanding Force J. /IWM

Top: HMS *Warspite* bombarding enemy batteries on D day. This famous battleship was completed in 1915 and took part in the Battle of Jutland. /IWM

Above: HMS *Roberts* – monitor – bombarding off the French coast on D day. HMS *Frobisher* in the background. /IWM

Above: USS *Texas*, flagship of Rear Admiral C. F. Bryant, USN. Bombarding Force C assigned to *Omaha* beach. /*IWM*

Below: USS *Nevada* – Bombarding Force A assigned to *Utah* beach. /*IWM*

Top: HMS *Scylla* – flagship of Rear Admiral Sir Philip Vian, Naval Commander Eastern Task Force. /IWM

Above: USS *Augusta* – flagship of Rear Admiral Alan G. Kirk, USN, Naval Commander Western Task Force. /IWM

Top: Free French Ship *Georges Leygues* assigned to Bombarding
Force C. /*IWM*

Above: USS *Arkansas*, the oldest battleship in the US Navy and
assigned to Bombarding Force C. /*IWM*

Below: A Hunt class destroyer, one of the many which performed valuable service, escorting the invasion convoys. /*IWM*

Bottom: An LCT (Rocket) fires a salvo. /*IWM*

Right: A view of *Utah* beach as seen from the aperture of a German gun position. /*IWM*

Bottom right: US Troops heading inland from *Utah* beach. /*IWM*

Above: A scene off *Gold* beach showing MT unloaded and waiting to move inland. /IWM

Below: A DD Tank after landing, with DUKWS and other transport in the background. The photo shows the immense amount of equipment required. /IWM

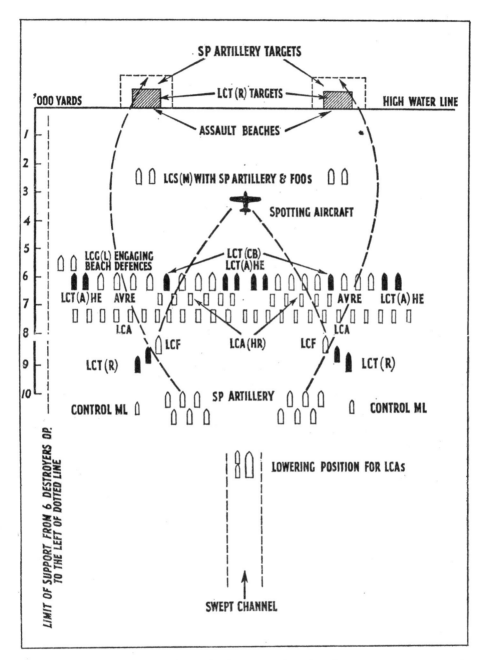

Operation Neptune. Typical deployment for the close range support of the left hand brigade of a divisional assault.

was engaged by HMS *Ajax* and, after twenty minutes of very accurate shooting, it was effectively put out of action.

The weather, as Admiral Vian was to write, was "unexpectedly severe for the launching of an operation of this type." It was as well that the lowering position was only seven miles off shore instead of eleven miles as at the American beaches. Even so the unfortunate troops in the landing craft were cold, wet and seasick before they reached the beaches, but despite the adverse conditions the timing of the assaults was remarkably accurate. Both senior officers of the assault groups, in consultation with the Army officers embarked, decided against launching the DD tanks off shore and they were carried right up to the beaches. They followed close on the heels of the Landing Craft Tank (Armoured Vehicle, Royal Engineers) carrying the demolition parties, who were the first ashore and for a time carried out their work of dismantling the beach obstacles, unsupported. The tide, under the influence of the strong wind, was rising half an hour ahead of schedule and the obstacles proved more numerous and heavier than expected; in consequence there was insufficient time to clear them before the arrival of the first wave of assault troops. Many landing craft were damaged by mines fixed to the uncleared obstacles, and failure to lay out kedge anchors in many cases resulted in their broaching to and encumbering the beaches against the arrival of subsequent waves. The troops landing on Jig sector met with an unpleasant surprise. The strong point at Le Hamel on the extreme right of the beach had survived the pre H-hour bombardments and the SP artillery of the support group failed to engage it as planned. It was bombarded by three destroyers but was protected from low trajectory fire from seaward, and it was not until 1600, after further shelling by Landing Craft Gun and Flak at close range that it was silenced and overrun.

Another position which offered stubborn resistance was sited at La Rivière, a mile east of King sector. Although the bombardment here had been more effective than at Le Hamel, the western end of the village was still intact and from it came withering fire as the troops came ashore. The strong point was ultimately silenced by a tank. West of La Rivière the defences were penetrated without great difficulty.

At 1050 and 1120 the reserve brigades were landed. By now

several passages had been cleared through the beach obstructions, seven exits were in use and traffic was moving well. With the arrival of reinforcements the assault gained momentum and by 2100 that night the town of Arromanches, the site selected for one of the Mulberry harbours, had been captured.

The task of securing certain important objectives had been entrusted to six British and one French Commandos. Number 47 Royal Marine Commando, Lieutenant-Colonel C. F. Phillips, RM, had been detailed to capture Port en Bessin, a very useful little harbour sheltered by two curved breakwaters, but which was very strongly defended from an attack from seaward, so it was planned to take it from the landward side. The Commando landed, not without difficulty, in Jig sector at 0930, nine miles east of its objective. Of its sixteen landing craft four were lost and eleven damaged and the Marines had fifty yards of water to wade through before reaching the beach; as a result they lost a lot of their equipment and all their radio sets. They were held up for most of the day at La Rosière, a short distance inland, but they eventually succeeded in taking it and in re-equipping themselves with captured German equipment. They resumed their westward march at 1945 and after another brush with the enemy reached a position south of Port en Bessin, where they dug in for the night. Fortunately the enemy was not aware of their presence and at daylight the next day, after an unsuccessful attempt to establish contact with US troops from *Omaha*, the Marines did succeed in arranging for gun support from HMS *Emerald* and form rocket-firing fighters of the Royal Air Force. Under cover of smoke shell, provided by a battery of 25 pounder guns in the vicinity of Arromanches, the assault went in and the port was captured, together with two German Flak ships in the harbour. This was an outstanding example of inter-service co-operation.

Earlier on, before the Commando landed, Admiral Vian visited *Gold* area in his flagship HMS *Scylla,* and assisted in the capture of Arromanches by firing forty rounds of 5.25 inch into its defences before returning to *Sword* area.

JUNO BEACH

Juno beach, four and a half miles long, ran eastward from *Gold* beach. It was divided into three sectors, Love, Mike and Nan and was distinguished by the extent of the rocky outcrop with which it was faced. On this account H-hour was delayed to 0735 in the Mike sector and 0745 in the Nan sector. Debouching into the sea in the Mike sector was the river Seulles and the whole beach was backed by sand dunes, except at the eastern end where a high sea wall had been built. The only battery facing *Juno* was one of four 3.9in guns at Beny sur Mer, three miles inland, but the Germans had established several strong points along the water front. However, these were manned by the 716th division containing a high proportion of conscript troops of Russian and Polish nationality, whose enthusiasm for combat was not very high.

Force 'J', under the command of Commodore G. N. Oliver, RN, in the headquarters ship HMS *Hilary*, was scheduled to reach the lowering position seven miles off *Juno* beach at 0550/6. In the van was Bombarding Squadron 'E', comprising the cruisers HMS *Belfast*, flagship of Rear-Admiral F. G. H. Dalrymple-Hamilton, *Diadem* and eleven destroyers, two of which were Canadian and one Free French manned. The Support Group comprising seven Landing Craft Gun (Large), eight Landing Craft Tank (Rocket), six Landing Craft Support (Large), six Landing Craft Flak and four regiments of SP Artillery, embarked in eight Landing Craft Tank (Armoured) and eight Landing Craft Tank (High Explosive), were included amongst the three Groups J1, J2 and J3 totalling 187 ships which made up the Assault Force. The passage of the Force through the swept channels although not interfered with by the enemy, was marked by navigational errors by which some of the ships of J1 Group used channels, to the west of the ones (7 and 8) allocated to them. This fortunately was not of great consequence except in the case of the Landing Craft Tank (Armoured Vehicle Royal Engineers) (AVRE) which were unable to make up the easting they had lost and keep to their schedule. Due to this and the heavy weather, it was found necessary to amend H-hour to 0745 in the Mike sector and 0755 in the Nan one. These progressive postponements meant that the landing craft would be obliged to touch down in the middle of the obstructions designed to destroy them.

It was off *Juno* beach that submarine X20 was performing her valuable marking duties and, these completed, she left the area and was towed back to Portsmouth. Both groups J1 and J2 had decided that the weather was too bad to allow the DD tanks to swim ashore, but the Senior Officer of Group J1 later revised his decision and launched his tanks 1,000 yards off shore. Eight were lost but the remainder made it to the beach in Mike sector between 0759 and 0810. The tanks in the Landing Craft Tank (Armoured Vehicle Royal Engineers), containing the demolition parties, did not touch down until 0816, six minutes after the infantry. Luckily the obstacles were more widely spaced and less formidable than on some of the other beaches for, despite strenuous efforts to make up for lost time, the tide rose too rapidly for much clearance to be achieved until after High Water. In Group J2 the landing in Nan sector went smoothly, the demolition parties landing at 0805, followed by the infantry at 0811 and the DD tanks a few minutes later. The landing craft incurred very few casualties on the way but many were damaged when attempting to withdraw to return to the lowering area.

Typical of the courage and initiative shown by the young officers in charge of the Landing Craft is the story of Midshipman Charles Fowler, aged 19, and First Lieutenant of an LCT carrying tanks of the 2nd Canadian Armoured Brigade. "As the vessel ran into the beaches it came under heavy fire from Germans hiding in a house close to the shore. The guns of the LCT replied but one gun suddenly jammed. The Commanding Officer rushed from the bridge to aid the gunner but was mortally wounded before he reached the gun. Midshipman Fowler took command of the craft and carried on although her steering gear was shot away. In the face of the continued heavy fire she unloaded her tanks. A mortar bomb landed on the deck of the LCT but before it could explode Leading Stoker J. Gamble of Colne, Lincolnshire, seized it and threw it back at the enemy. It exploded against a nest of Germans. The casualties in the LCT were mounting – two of the crew were killed and three wounded – but Midshipman Fowler finished the unloading of his craft and then found that she was struck on the sands. He went ashore to get assistance and managed to persuade the driver of an Army bulldozer to help him off with a shove and a heave of his powerful vehicle. There was still a strong wind blowing, the sea was rough and the lightly built landing craft had no steering gear working. Undaunted, Midshipman Fowler, who had never before had command of a vessel, headed the craft for England. Steering with main engines he reached the south coast some hours later."[7]

Despite the pre H-hour bombardment, many of the German defences had survived unscathed, and they held their fire until the troops began to disembark when they found themselves under shell and mortar fire as well as close range weapons and small fire arms. The opposition was heaviest in the centre of each sector, but the Canadians with great élan and the support of the tanks managed to overwhelm and neutralise most of the strong points within an hour of landing. The bombarding ships and the support groups also did excellent work, the ships of the latter closing to within 1,000 yards while the regiments of SP artillery, in spite of the difficult weather conditions, did some remarkably accurate shooting. An unfortunate incident occurred when a passing Typhoon aircraft encountered a salvo of rockets fired from a Landing Craft Tank (Rocket) in mid-flight and was destroyed.

A German writer describing the assault says, "Such German strong points as were still intact continued to resist, but as a fighting unit the 716th Division had been smashed by the murderous aerial and naval bombardment."[8]

Nine Landing Craft Assault (Hedgerow) had been allotted to each assault group; those attached to Group J1 had all foundered except one, but those with Group J2 reached their firing positions safely and on time and launched their 216 60-lb bombs with very good effect.

Number 48 Royal Marine Commando, Lieutenant-Colonel J. L. Moulton, RM, had been given the task of clearing up the beach defences and establishing a link with troops landing on *Sword* – Queen beach seven miles east of *Juno* – Nan beach. The Commando landed at 0830 from six Landing Craft Infantry (Small); though each carried 90 men, their wooden hulls afforded no protection and they received considerable damage through striking beach obstacles. In fact, two of them were prevented from beaching at all and their occupants had to swim ashore, some being drowned by the weight of the equipment they carried. On landing, the Marines met intense machine gun and mortar fire from an enemy strong point at St. Aubin, which had been by-

84

passed by the first wave of assault troops and they lost half their fighting strength. However, the Commando succeeded in clearing the beach and began to advance eastward, hoping to join up with Number 41 Commando working westward from Lion sur Mer. On reaching Langrune, a mile east of the landing, it found the enemy very strongly established in a series of blockhouses and buildings in the village, the approaches to which from both east and west were heavily mined and protected on the sea side by a concrete wall four feet thick and five feet six inches high, as well as trenches and barbed wire. It was clear that without artillery and tanks the strong point could not be taken. Fighting continued all day with the help of first a Centaur and later a Sherman tank. At 2100, however, the attack had to be called off and the Commando redeployed to meet the threat of a German armoured counter-attack, which fortunately did not materialise. The next morning the attack on Langrune was resumed, the German position was gradually infiltrated and eventually the defenders surrendered. At about 1130/7 the Commando was able to continue its eastward march.

At 1133/6 the first craft carrying the reserve brigade group touched down on Nan sector and seventeen minutes later had disembarked. At 1715 the headquarters ship HMS *Hilary* shifted berth closer inshore and Admiral Vian, who had been touring the beaches in a US Coastguard cutter during the afternoon, returned to HMS *Scylla* which then anchored near by, preparatory to a conference of Flag Officers and Commodores which took place at 1800 and became a daily feature of the operation. The *Scylla* subsequently returned to *Sword* area. Meanwhile Group L1 of the Follow-up Force 'L', with thirteen Landing Ship Tanks carrying General Montgomery's 21 Army Group Headquarters and the 51st (H) Division together with HMS *Northway,* a Landing Ship Dock, loaded with DUKWS and four pre-loaded coasters, had arrived and anchored, but despite the accumulation of ships in the area there was no enemy air activity until 0150/7.

SWORD BEACH

The easternmost of the beaches in the Baie de la Seine chosen for the assault was the one named *Sword.* It extended six miles east of

St. Aubin sur Mer as far as the estuary of the River Orne, on the west side of which lay the Caen Canal. It was subdivided into sectors Oboe, Peter, Queen and Roger, but only Queen was to be used for the initial landing. The anchorage was well within range of a German battery of three 16in guns known to be sited on the coast to the north of Le Havre, but there need have been no anxiety on this score, had it been known that it had already been put out of action following a raid some days previously by aircraft of Bomber Command of the Royal Air Force. However, it was believed that three 11in and some thirty-five 6in guns were also sited in the Le Havre area.

The rocky outcrop which fronted *Juno* beach continued across that of *Sword,* the beaches of which were narrower. At the estuary of the Orne a large sandbank extended about a mile out to sea and, as the western sectors of the beach were backed by low cliffs, it had been decided to land on a single brigade front. As regards artillery, a battery of four 3.9in guns was sited a mile inland on Queen sector but the guns of a battery of 6in guns, believed to be located on the coast at Ouistreham, had been removed and another four, a mile inland, were not manned. The beach defences were not quite as formidable as at the other three beaches to the west.

Force 'S', commanded by Rear-Admiral A. G. Talbot in the head-quarters ship HMS *Largs,* began sailing from Spithead at 0945/5, being joined by Bombarding Force 'D' off the Isle of Wight. This last, under the command of Rear-Admiral W. R. Patterson with his flag in the cruiser HMS *Mauritius,* had been specially strengthened to deal with the enemy batteries at Le Havre and comprised the battleships HMS *Warspite* and *Ramillies,* the monitor *Roberts,* the cruisers *Frobisher, Arethusa, Danae* and the ORP (Okręt Rzeczypospolitej Polskiej – Ship of the Polish Republic) *Dragon* with thirteen destroyers. The Support Force comprised three Landing Craft Gun (Large), five Landing Craft Tank (Rocket), three Landing Craft Support (Large), four Landing Craft Flak, and eight regiments of SP artillery in eight Landing Craft Tank (Armoured). They were included amongst the ships of Assault Group S3 which, together with Assault Groups S1 and S2, made up Force 'S', totalling 285 ships.

Force 'S' was the only one of the five Assault Forces to encounter any enemy forces. It proceeded down swept channels 9 and 10 without incident and the bombarding ships HMS *Warspite, Ramillies, Roberts* and *Arethusa* anchored in their bombarding positions at the southern end of channel 10 and opened fire. Meanwhile, HMS *Scylla, Mauritius, Danae, Frobisher* and ORP *Dragon* had taken up their positions in the swept loop joining channels 9 and 10 and the Headquarters ship HMS *Largs,* together with Group S2 and a convoy of DD tanks, were entering the lowering area. In accordance with the plan, aircraft were laying a smoke screen to the east of the Assault area to shield the force from the batteries at Le Havre. Suddenly, without warning, at 0530 three German torpedo boats of the 5th T/B flotilla based on Le Havre emerged from behind the smoke screen and delivered an attack. Two torpedoes passed between the *Warspite* and the *Ramillies,* whilst a third would have hit HMS *Largs* but for the prompt action of her Captain who had put his engines full speed astern and the torpedo passed ahead. A fourth torpedo hit the Norwegian destroyer *Svenner* amidships and she broke in two and sank, most of her crew being rescued. In all, the enemy fired fifteen torpedoes. The *Warspite* engaged the enemy with her secondary armament using radar control and so did the *Ramillies, Mauritius* and *Arethusa,* but the torpedo boats returned safely to base. The 15th German Patrol Flotilla, however, came under heavy fire and one of their number was sunk after striking a mine.

The enemy batteries east of the Orne concentrated their fire on the bombarding ships and a battery of four 6in guns at Bennerville became so troublesome that the *Warspite* was obliged to shift berth although she did not receive a direct hit. By 0930 the main batteries appeared to have been silenced, but to keep them that way required periodical attention throughout the day.

H-hour for the assault on *Sword* – Queen beach was 0725 and anxiously awaiting the arrival of the main force were the 6th Airborne Division under Major-General Richard Gale, which had been parachuted during the night into the area east of the River Orne, with the object of capturing intact the bridges on the only through road over the Orne and the Canal from the sea to the town of Caen, the capture of which was a primary objective. Despite landing difficulties, the Division had succeeded in its tasks, but German counter-attacks could be expected in strength in this vital area, hence the need to reinforce it as soon as possible. HMS *Mauritius* and *Arethusa* had orders to provide gunfire support to this Division and this they did most successfully, enabling the troops to withstand the heavy enemy pressure which now began to build up.

As on the other beaches, the spearhead of the landing was to be the DD tanks and, to ensure that they landed at the correct place, submarine X23 was stationed off sector Queen to guide them in. Although weather conditions were not at all favourable, it was decided to launch them 5,000 yards from the beach and of the 40 tanks carried 34 were launched successfully. Two subsequently sank and one was rammed by an LCT (AVRE) but the surviving 31 touched down at 0730 and gave invaluable fire support to the succeeding waves of infantry. Once again the enemy weapons were so mounted as to be unable to fire to seaward and the troops were often misled into thinking that they had been silenced by the pre H-hour bombardment, whereas they were only waiting for targets to cross their line of sight. All the LCT (AVRE) except one, which was hit by a mortar shell which detonated the Bangalore torpedoes mounted on one of her tanks, landed their tanks almost simultaneously with the arrival of the DD tanks. In general, the opposition was slight, except on the eastern flank, and the obstacles much as expected. The Landing Craft Tank Armoured with their 95mm guns, and the Landing Craft Tank (Concrete Buster) touched down on the flanks five minutes after H-hour but two were severely hit and became a total loss.

At 0750 the first Free French troops to return to their homeland came ashore and suffered casualties from anti-tank guns and mortar fire. The last groups of the assault brigade touched down at 0943, only 18 minutes behind schedule, and the intermediate brigade followed soon afterwards, but the landing of the reserve brigade had to be delayed as by now congestion on the beach began to build up and soon reached chronic proportions.

"Except for initial loses, the assault on *Sword* beach went forward speedily, meeting little sustained opposition. The landings were so successful that many men coming in minutes after the first wave were surprised to find only sniper fire. They saw the beaches shrouded in smoke, nursing orderlies working among the wounded, flail tanks detonating mines, burning tanks and vehicles littering the shore line, but nowhere was there the slaughter they had expected."[9] Meanwhile the weather, the obstacles, mines and mortar fire were playing havoc with the landing craft, seven of which had been destroyed by midday. However, as a result of heroic exertions by the young officers commanding them, and of their crews by dint of what Admiral Talbot was to call, "grim determination and good seamanship", many were extracted from the perilous positions in which they found themselves, those getting off first lending a helping hand to the ones still aground. At 1535 Admiral Talbot landed to see for himself how things were going. As he set foot ashore, seven Ju88 aircraft strafed the beaches and mortar fire was continuous. He found 24 major landing craft still stranded and much congestion on the beaches, due to traffic blocks on the roads leading inland from the beach exits. On returning to HMS *Largs* he arranged for working parties from the fleet to be landed to assist with clearing up the beaches.

Number 41 Royal Marine Commando, Lieutenant-Colonel T. M. Gray, RM, had crossed the Channel in five LCI(S) and touched down at 0845 300 yards west of its correct landing position at Lion-sur-Mer in Peter sector. It was greeted with shell and mortar fire and the evidence of the toll this had taken on the troops which had landed there earlier. However, the force managed to clear the beach quickly but was held up at Lion-sur-Mer by the enemy. Despite a two hour bombardment by destroyers during the afternoon, the position was not taken until the following morning after which the Commando was able to resume its westward march to join up with No. 48 Commando advancing from *Juno* beach. On reaching Petit Enfer, it met up with Number 46 Royal Marine Commando, the original objectives of which had been changed and which had been detailed to capture this village instead. It had done this successfully, taking 65 prisoners.

Number 45 Royal Marine Commando, Lieutenant-Colonel N. C. Ries, RM, landed at La Brèche, on the outskirts of Ouistreham, at 0910 and moved east to the support of the 6th Airborne Division. Later it became involved in heavy fighting in the vicinity of Franceville, where German mobile guns hidden in a wood south of the village were giving a lot of trouble.

At 2250, in order to protect the crowded anchorage from expected enemy attack, smoke cover was provided and ten minutes later enemy aircraft were reported approaching. Their arrival, unfortunately, synchronised with that of 300 troop carriers and towed gliders carrying reinforcements for the 6th Airborne Division. This was a situation which Admiral Ramsay had foreseen and tried unsuccessfully to prevent. Inevitably some ships opened fire and ignored repeated signals to Cease Fire and, as a result, at least two British aircraft were shot down. At Admiral Vian's request, all future airborne operations of this nature were confined to daylight hours.

It would have been expecting too much to hope that all the assault groups would reach their destinations exactly as planned and, as has been related, this was not the case, but the success of the first phase of Operation Neptune was never really in doubt. Admiral Ramsay says, "The outstanding fact was that despite the unfavourable weather, in every main essential the plan was carried out as written."[10] Total casualties of craft amounted to 304, of which about 50 per cent were due to beach obstacles fitted with Teller mines. By the close of D-day in the British-Canadian area 70,472 troops of the Assault and Follow-up formations had been landed and casualties amounted to 1,848, a figure far smaller than expected.

Most noticeable had been the feebleness of the enemy's air opposition and the absence of serious attacks on shipping and the beaches. This was due of course to the weakness of the Luftwaffe, but no chances had been taken. Throughout the assault, continuous cover was maintained by nine squadrons of fighters. Six of these were Spitfires, providing low cover, while three of Thunderbolts gave high cover. In addition, a continuous patrol over the shipping lanes and assault forces was maintained by four squadrons of Lightnings.

"By the end of D-day", wrote Admiral Ramsay, "immediate anxiety was felt on only one count, whether the weather would improve sufficiently quickly to enable the build-up to start as planned."[11]

Notes
1   Report of Naval Commander, Eastern Task Force.
2   Friedrich Ruge, *Rommel Face au Débarquement 1944*.
3   W. H. Pugsley, *Saints, Devils and Ordinary Seamen*.
4   Quoted by Chester Wilmot in *The Struggle for Europe*.

5 Report of Naval Commander, Force 'U'.
6 Samuel Morison, *History of US Naval Operations in World War II,* Vol XI.
7 Gordon Holman, *Stand By to Beach.*
8 Paul Carrell, *Invasion – They're Coming.*
9 Cornelius Ryan, *The Longest Day.*
10 ANCFX Report on Neptune, Vol I.
11 Ibid.

Chapter Six

The Build-Up

DEFENCE OF THE ASSAULT AREA

The defence of the assault area off Normandy presented a problem different from that with which previous amphibious operations had to contend. To begin with a far larger number of ships and craft were involved, the anchorages were closer together, and the Allies possessed overwhelming air superiority. Attacks within the area by U-boats and surface craft other than fast motor boats were considered unlikely on account of mines, and air attack on a large scale was also ruled out. It was, therefore, decided to adopt a static system of defence, as in any case there was very little room for ships to manoeuvre.

The responsibility for dealing with enemy forces in the English Channel outside the assault area rested with the Commanders-in-Chief Portsmouth and Plymouth and the Vice-Admiral, Dover, but there was close co-ordination between them and Admiral Ramsay.

The Navy Task Force Commanders of the Western and Eastern areas each made their dispositions for guarding their respective flanks. Admiral Kirk divided the American area into eight defence sub-areas known as Mountain, Hickory and Elder to seaward, with Prairie, Vermont, Kansas, Oregon and Ohio in the south and east (*see Map 3*). A line known as the Dixie line ran from a point seven miles north of Port en Bessin on the dividing line between the Western and Eastern areas, to a point three miles 026 degrees from the St. Marcouf Islands. He stationed a division of destroyers in area Prairie and established radar pickets in the northern parts of

92

areas Kansas and Ohio. A line from the north-western end of the Dixie line ran south-south-west to the northern limit of *Utah* beach and, known as the Mason line, was patrolled by MTBs. Later on, as the result of experience, MTBs and Steam Gunboats were stationed in the north-west part of area Mountain, where they were in a good position to intercept enemy forces rounding Cap Barfleur. So skilfully were these patrols handled that, after a few attempts at penetration, the enemy 'E' boats left the area severely alone.

In the Eastern Task Force area Admiral Vian established two areas north of the assault area, the dividing line between them being a line drawn due north from St. Aubin as far as latitude 49 degrees 40′N (*see Map 3*). The eastern area, known as Tunny, covered the mouth of the Seine and was considered the most dangerous one since land echoes might interfere with radar warning. The western area, known as Pike, extended to longitude 0 degrees 40′W, the dividing line between the American and British areas. A defence line six miles off shore and parallel to it was occupied each night by minesweepers anchored five cables apart. From the eastern end of this line another one ran due south to the shore and was known as the Trout line. It was manned nightly by Landing Craft Gun and Landing Craft Flak anchored 200 yards apart. When, during July and August, the enemy employed explosive motor boats, human torpedoes and other ingenious devices in an attempt to penetrate the defences, the Trout line assumed very great importance.

Two or three divisions of MTBs were stationed to the northward of the north-west corner of the defence perimeter, while two or three sub-divisions of destroyers patrolled north and south in the western part of area Tunny. A Captain of Patrols was in charge of the defence organisation and he operated from a destroyer or frigate under way but stopped in the inner defence area. At first smoke was employed to screen ships in the inner anchorage, but as the enemy stepped up his minelaying activities, the importance of marking where the mines fell brought about a modification in the procedure for the use of smoke.

The co-ordination of all the measures taken for the defence of the Eastern area was centred in the operations room of HMS *Scylla*, which was anchored each night about two and a half miles inside the defence line and near its north-eastern corner.

By day, corvettes, trawlers and sometimes destroyers patrolled to seaward of the inner defence area but the enemy made no attempt during daylight to interfere with the progress of the build up and, as the nights were short, his opportunities for offensive action were limited.

NAVAL GUN SUPPORT

As the troops gradually fought their way inland and enlarged the beachhead they had gained on D-day, the work of the bombarding ships changed in character and became more selective. To the west, the whole of the Cotentin Peninsula was within range of naval guns, but the batteries at St. Marcouf, Crisbecq and Quinville continued to hold out stubbornly and were not finally silenced until captured by ground forces. After some initial difficulties due to casualties and communication failures, the shore fire control parties (SFCPs) in the American sector and the forward observers bombardment (FOBs) in the British area established good contact with the bombarding ships and calls for fire support from the armies were met promptly and effectively. Spotting by fighter aircraft was also employed with good effect. "By common consent," wrote Admiral Ramsay, "the shooting was uniformly good and it is considered that the initial advances of the armies were helped in no small measure by the naval supporting fire."[1] There is ample confirmation of this from German sources. The War Diary of Naval Group, West, for June 20 contains the following entry: "It is generally accepted that the intended offensive of the German Army has no chance of success unless the exceedingly effective shelling by enemy naval guns of our own land units can be prevented. The German Navy is not capable of making an attack. The Luftwaffe which is numerically just as inferior also refuses to attack naval targets by day. As the battleships move away from the coastal area at night there appears to be no solution." After the war Field Marshal von Rundstedt told the late Sir Basil Liddell Hart, "Besides the interference from the air, the fire of your battleships was a main factor in hampering our counterstroke."[2] It was the ability of the heavy guns of the battleships to deliver a 2000 lb shell at a range of up to 15 miles which seems to have taken the German Army by surprise. Admiral Morison cites an instance when on June 8 the guns of the battleship *Nevada*, with 70 rounds of 14 inch shell at a range of 23,500 yards, wiped out a concentration of 90 tanks and 20 vehicles.

Prior to the bombardment of Cherbourg, an account of which appears later, enemy shore batteries did not score a single hit on any of the bombarding ships. This fact has been attributed to the use of smoke, the jamming of the enemy's radar and the effect of the bombardment itself.

NAVAL ACTIVITY JUNE 7 TO 16

Whilst the German Army Command in the West was trying to obtain Hitler's permission for the use of additional armoured divisions with which to counter-attack the Allied armies in Normandy, Grand Admiral Dönitz was implementing his plans for his surface forces and U-boats to intercept the Allied convoys which he knew would flood across the Channel in support of the invasion. Naval Group West had drawn up a plan of action for its surface forces as follows:

(i) The 5th and 9th MTB flotillas based on Cherbourg were to carry out minelaying and torpedo attacks in the assault area, particularly that part in which United States forces were operating.

(ii) The 2nd and 4th MTB flotillas operating from Boulogne were to lay mines off Ouistreham and carry out torpedo attacks in the Eastern Task Force area using Le Havre and Cherbourg as convenient.

(iii) The 8th MTB flotilla operating from Ostend was to patrol the eastern part of the Channel.

Later on, on June 11, the 6th MTB flotilla was moved from the Baltic to the invasion area.

The implementation of these plans was frustrated to a large extent by the strength of the Allied defence and also by a shortage of torpedoes at Le Havre, but Dönitz had one weapon up his sleeve on which he pinned great hopes and this was the 'oyster' or 'pressure' mine, which Hitler had forbidden him to use before the invasion, in case its secret should be discovered and the Allies should lay them in the Baltic where the training of new types of U-boats was in progress. There were two types of these mines, fired by the change in hydrostatic pressure which occurred when a ship passed over them at speed. One of them was virtually unsweepable and the other only when the weather was suitable. A large stock was available and there is little doubt that had they been laid in the approaches to the ports from which the invasion convoys were to sail, they would have been a considerable embarrassment to the Allies and might have caused serious losses. As it was, they were to place a great strain on the counter-measures which the Allies were obliged to take. Interspersed amongst the 'oyster' mines were those operated by acoustic and/or magnetic pistols and these were fitted with delay action mechanisms and also antisweeping devices which destroyed the sweep. All in all therefore, a very heavy load was placed on the Allied mine sweepers during the post-invasion period and especially on those of the inshore type which lacked the accommodation and cooking facilities available in larger types. No praise is too high for the men who manned these little ships.

Although the new mines came as a surprise to the Allies, during the first ten days of their use in the British area, only eleven vessels, which included the hospital carriers *Dinard* and *St. Julien* and the minesweeper HMS *Rattlesnake,* were mined but not sunk, and the Trinity House vessel *Alert* was mined and sank. In the American area, however, the losses were more severe. The destroyer USS *Glennon* and the destroyer escort USS *Rich* were sunk by mines on June 8 and no less than 30 mines were detonated in the boat channels leading from the transport area to *Utah* beach, two of the minesweepers being lost and 25 other ships and craft damaged. The *Omaha* area, however, received far less attention from enemy minelayers.

Fortunately a mislay by an enemy aircraft resulted in an 'oyster' mine being discovered in the ruins of some houses in Rivabella, behind *Sword* beach, and the secret of its operation was soon discovered. It was found that, provided the speed of a ship passing over it did not exceed four knots, it would not be triggered off.

The first night after the invasion was comparatively quiet, enemy activity generally being on a moderate scale. At 0110/7 the trawler *Grenadier* destroyed an enemy aircraft and, just after dawn, the headquarters ship HMS *Bulolo* was hit by a 250lb phosphorous

96

bomb which killed one naval and two RAF officers and one naval rating without, however, impairing the ship's operating efficiency.

At 0336/7, 'E' boats on a minelaying expedition were engaged by MTBs of the British 29th and 55th flotillas off Le Havre and one of the enemy aircraft was damaged. Off *Omaha* beach Admiral Hall's flagship, *USS Ancon*, was near-missed by bombs and one enemy aircraft was destroyed. The destroyer USS *Meredith*, on patrol off the St. Marcouf Islands, was hit by a glider bomb at 0152/8 and subsequently sank.

Outside the assault area enemy reaction was more vigorous. With some sixteen convoys and about the same number of landing craft ones at sea at any one time, contact with the enemy was highly probable and casualties inevitable. All the same, whenever an attack took place it was stoutly resisted and losses were comparatively light, having regard to the large number of vessels at risk.

On the night of June 7/8 seven actions took place between 'E' boats from the 5th and 9th flotillas from Cherbourg and Allied patrols off Cap Barfleur. Boats of the the 9th flotilla reached the Spout and attacked a convoy of LCTs and LCI(L)s, escorted by MT903, which put up a very spirited defence against a superior enemy in which she was assisted by fire from the ships of the convoy. Two LCTs were lost and another damaged before the enemy withdrew. On their return to Cherbourg two 'E' boats were mined and sank.

The next night, June 8/9, 'E' boats again penetrated to the Spout and attacked convoy EBC3 of seventeen ships, but were driven off by the escort HMS *Watchman*. To the east of Cap Barfleur another group of 'E' boats attacked convoy ECMI of fifteen MT ships and sixteen LSTs, two of the last named, LSTs 314 and 376 being sunk. HMS *Beagle* rescued 250 survivors. The most noteworthy event of this night, however, was the sinking of two German destroyers which, with one other, had been reported leaving the Gironde on D-day and which had put into Brest after being attacked by Beaufighters of the RAF. The destroyers HMS *Oribi*, *Offa*, *Onslaught*, *Scorpion* and *Scourge* had been ordered to patrol to the west of the Spout in anticipation of an attack by the German ships, while north of Ushant, the Commander-in-Chief, Plymouth, had stationed the 10th destroyer flotilla, comprising HMS *Tartar* (Commander B. Jones, RN, Senior Officer), *Ashanti, Haida, Huron,*

Eskimo, Javelin and ORP *Blyscawica* and *Piorun*. The three German destroyers, comprising the *Z.24* and *Z.32*, the former Dutch destroyer *Gerard Callonburgh* and a fourth ship, the *Elbing* were ordered to leave Brest for a sortie against Allied shipping when, at 0120/9, they were sighted and engaged by 10th Flotilla. In the ensuing action the *Gerard Callonburgh* was sunk, the *Z.32* driven ashore on the Ile de Bas, where she became a total wreck, while the heavily damaged *Z.24* and the *Elbing* managed to escape and reach Brest. Ships of the 14th Escort Group picked up 141 survivors the following day. This action effectively disposed of the threat to Allied shipping offered by the only German destroyers in the area.

During the next few days the enemy 'E' boats continued their attacks and frequent actions took place, in which losses and damage were suffered by both sides. On the night of June 9/10 four 'E' boats of the 2nd MTB flotilla from Boulogne, after having successfully attacked a northbound convoy, sank the British coasters *Dungrange* and *Brackenfield,* both loaded with ammunition, in the Spout, only two survivors from the latter being picked up. The following night the frigate HMS *Halstead,* had her bows blown off by a torpedo, while two tugs towing Whale units, a rescue tug and the United States Tug *Partridge,* were all sunk. On the night of June 11/12 HMS *Talybont* damaged two 'E' boats which, however, succeeded in torpedoing and sinking a Phoenix unit destined for Mulberry 'A' harbour. The night of June 12/13 was the last in which the 'E' boats were to operate in any strength and their luck was out for they failed to get in any attacks and they lost three of their number to aircraft when returning to Boulogne early on June 13. An 'R' boat which came to their assistance was also sunk.

On June 14 a concentration of 'E' boats was reported in Le Havre and Admiral Ramsay requested Bomber Command of the RAF to attack them. Eighteen Mosquito night fighters and 335 Lancaster bombers carried out the attack which was delivered just before dusk. A total of 1,026 tons of bombs were dropped, including 22 of 12,000lb of a special type. The torpedo boats *Falke, Jaguar* and *Moewe,* together with ten 'E' boats, two 'R' boats, fifteen minesweepers and patrol craft, three landing craft, a gun carrier, and five tugs were sunk. Four 'E' and four 'R' boats were badly damaged and torpedo boat *T.28* and eight minor craft slightly

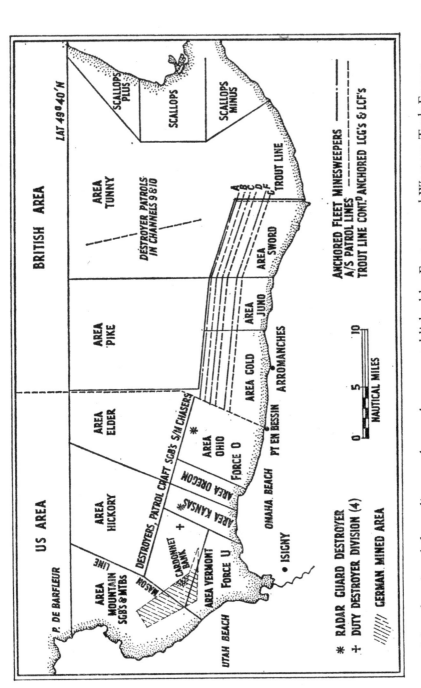

Map showing defence lines and patrol areas established by Eastern and Western Task Forces.

damaged. Admiral Krancke's diary records: "The attack on Havre is a catastrophe. Losses are extremely heavy. It will hardly be possible to carry out the operations planned with the remaining forces . . . Naval situation in Seine Bay has completely altered since yesterday: attack on Havre and increasing difficulties in supplying Cherbourg by land and sea." Admiral Ruge refers to Krancke's "great annoyance" in consequence of the attack, because the A/A guns had been ordered not to open fire as some German aircraft were to use some new form of weapons.[3]

The following night, June 15/16, similar treatment was meted out to the harbour of Boulogne with equally satisfactory results and, in consequence, German 'E' boat activity in the Channel from now on was confined to minelaying sorties.

On every night except one (June 26/27) the assault was subjected to a series of attacks by single, low-flying aircraft, some of which dropped bombs but most of them mines of the 'oyster' type. As many as 50 of these sorties would be made in one night. The frigate HMS *Lawford* and the SS *Charles Morgan* were sunk by bombs on the night of June 8/9 and 9/10 respectively. The next night five ships were damaged including, as already mentioned, HMS *Bulolo,* but these losses were not as serious as those which resulted from the minelaying activities.

U-BOAT ACTIVITY

As part of the counter-invasion measures the German Navy had formed a group of 36 U-boats known as the 'Landwirte' Group, the task of which was to attack Allied shipping supporting the invasion. Only seven of the group were schnorkel fitted and six of these sailed from Brest on D-day to operate in an area roughly halfway between the Needles and Cap de la Hague. The probability of this had been foreseen by Admiral Ramsay and he had arranged for Coastal Command of the RAF to institute what was described as "a solid wall of air patrols" over the south-western approaches. These were so effective that, in the first 48 hours, 33 sightings of U-boats were reported, 22 of which resulted in attacks. Two of the 'Landwirte' Group, U.955 and U.970, were sunk and seven others damaged and obliged to return to harbour. Although the schnorkel conferred the advantage of allowing the U-boat to use its diesel engines whilst remaining submerged, it restricted the speed of the boat and it was found that the long period of submergence had a distressing effect on the crews. Between June 8 and 12 four of those without schnorkel were sunk and the remainder were ordered to return to Brest with instructions that they were only to be used in the event of an Allied landing in the Bay of Biscay.

Asdic conditions in the Channel were not good and in consequence the A/S escort groups did not achieve many kills during the immediate post-invasion period, although their patrol areas were adjusted in the light of intelligence received of U-boat activity. It was not until June 15 that the U-boats achieved their first success, when HMS *Mourne* of the 5th Escort Group was torpedoed and blew up 45 miles north of Ushant. That evening HMS *Blackwood* was also torpedoed 20 miles north-north-west of Cap de la Hague and sank whilst being towed back to Portland. Nevertheless the efficiency of the Allied anti-submarine measures is demonstrated by the fact that for the first three weeks after the invasion, not a single merchant ship or landing craft fell a victim to U-boat attack.

CONVOY OPERATIONS

Admiral Ramsay had drawn up a detailed programme of convoy movements between British ports and the assault area covering the first three days after the invasion, after which it was expected that a regular rhythm of movement would develop. Unfortunately the Build-up Control Organisation (BUCO) proved unequal to its task and some difficulty was experienced in establishing a smooth flow of shipping. The immense task of the Build-up was not merely a question of Cross Channel traffic, although at first this undoubtedly accounted for the greater part of it, but a considerable quantity of shipping destined for Normandy was arriving in British ports from across the Atlantic and this had to be dovetailed into the Cross Channel traffic. Admiral Ramsay paid tribute to the work of the officers and men of the hundreds of merchant ships and coasters which took part in the Build-up. "It was not only in the waters of the assault area and the 'Spout' that merchant ships were exposed to danger," he wrote; "wherever they were, risks from U-boat, mines and air had to be faced. In addition those passing the Dover Straits were frequently shelled by enemy cross-channel batteries.

These batteries were responsible for the loss of two ships and damaged three others during the course of the month (June)."[4]

The eight convoys, comprising 98 ships, scheduled to arrive in the assault area on D + 1 day did so on time but the continuing unfavourable weather restricted the rate of unloading. Nevertheless, taking everything into consideration, what was achieved during the immediate post-invasion period was, as Admiral Ramsay has recorded, "really remarkable". The tonnage handled daily into France is estimated to have been equal to one-third of the United Kingdom's normal import capacity (*See Appendices VII and VIII*). During the first week, the daily average number of ships and craft arriving off the assault area was: 25 Liberty ships, 38 Coasters, 40 Landing Ships Tank, 75 Landing Craft Tank, 9 Personnel ships and 20 Landing Craft Infantry (Large). The identification, unloading, marshalling and sailing of such a large quantity of shipping was in itself a gigantic problem, which was not made any easier by the weather.

VISIT OF THE SUPREME COMMANDER

In the afternoon of June 7 General Eisenhower, accompanied by Admiral Ramsay, boarded the fast minelayer HMS *Apollo* at Portsmouth for a visit to the assault beaches to see for themselves how things were going. On passage they came across a number of landing craft and barges which had broken adrift and steps were taken to have them rounded up. On arrival they found the assault forces were suffering from a shortage of armoured vehicles, occasioned through the loss of the DD tanks referred to in the last chapter. The Supreme Commander was disturbed too, by the gap which still existed in the Carentan estuary between the forces landed on the *Utah* and *Omaha* beaches. Fortunately, the Germans were not in a position to exploit this gap before it was closed. Ramsay found that conditions for unloading at *Omaha* beach were hampered by a nasty lop but at the other beaches they were improving steadily, but there was still a lot of work to be done in salvaging stranded landing craft.

During the course of the same day General Montgomery crossed to France in the destroyer HMS *Faulknor*, and set up his tactical headquarters at Creully, ten miles west of Caen. General Omar

Bradley also crossed the Channel and conferred wth Admirals Kirk and Moon on board USS *Augusta*.

THE GOOSEBERRIES

It was urgently necessary to provide protection as soon as possible for the small craft operating off the beaches and the arrival of the first 'Corncob' convoy, composed of blockships, at 1230 on D + 1, was most opportune. It included the old cruiser HMS *Durban,* ship of the Senior Officer, Captain L. B. Hill, DSO, OBE, RN, who was responsible for planting the Gooseberries, as the blockships were called, in their correct positions. The others were the former radio-target battleship HMS *Centurion*, the French battleship *Courbet*, the Dutch Cruiser HMNS *Sumatra*, together with 31 British and 25 United States merchant ships, making a total of 60. They were to be planted in five groups, one to the eastward of St. Martin de Varreville and the other four to the northward of St. Laurent, Arromanches, Courseulles and Ouistreham. All ships except the *Courbet*, which had to be towed, crossed the Channel under their own steam. They had been prepared for sinking by having ten pound charges of amatol fixed on either side in each hold three feet below the water line; in the warships heavier charges were used. Despite enemy gunfire and the fact that many of the shore navigational marks were obscured by the fog of war the ships were sunk as planned, the work being completed by D + 4. The Gooseberries off St. Laurent and Arromanches were subsequently incorporated into the Mulberry harbours, and the position of one off Ouistreham was altered at Admiral Talbot's request so as to give greater protection from the north-west, and in consequence less from the north-east, a decision which he subsequently had cause to regret. The Gooseberries fulfilled all expectations and proved invaluable in providing shelter for ferry craft and as bases for maintenance and repair work, as well as accommodation for the men employed on this work. It took the Germans quite a time to appreciate their function and an entry in Group West's Diary for June 27 (D + 21) refers to the probability that they were ships which had been mined.

Unloading Problems

At all beaches initial difficulties were encountered in unloading the large quantity of vehicles, stores and ammunition which now began to arrive in increasing amounts. Admiral Ramsay's orders contained specific instructions that Landing Ships Tank were not to be dried out except in an emergency, but it was soon found that even when beached at High Water, the depth of water at the end of the ramp was too great for vehicles to be able to drive off. When this was reported the order was rescinded and it was found that no harm came to the LSTs or to the Coasters when allowed to dry out. On *Utah* beach the great range of the tide and the gentle slope of the beach favoured this drying out procedure, which was used for Landing Barges Vehicle, Landing Craft Mechanised, in addition to LSTs and LCTs and Coasters, and the procedure, became standard from D + 3 onwards, resulting in a greatly improved rate of discharge. However, delays in discharging Coasters persisted until D + 10 when a joint Navy-Army conference was called to solve the problem.

On *Omaha* beach, littered with the debris of the previous day's heavy fighting, and still under fire from German batteries and mortars, unloading fell badly behind schedule, much to Admiral Hall's concern. Matters were not helped when the Army insisted on certain priorities for unloading and since, due to a mistake, the manifests of the cargoes had been sent to the British area, an impossible situation arose. It was solved after Admiral Ramsay visited the beachhead on June 10 and ordered that ships be unloaded without reference to priorities, which must be left to take care of themselves. General Bradley subsequently concurred in this view. Group O4 of 134 ships, which should have arrived at *Omaha* at 1830 on D-day and Group O5 of 80 ships due at 0700 on D + 1 were both twelve hours late due to the weather, and, as the first of the personnel convoys of the Follow-up Force 'B', consisting of four transports, was also due on that day, the problem became acute. One of the transports, the USS *Susan B. Anthony*, was mined at 0820/7 while approaching the anchorage and sank one and a half hours later, but all the personnel on board were rescued. Under the forceful leadership of Captain Lorenzo S. Sabin, USN, the problems were gradually overcome and by D + 9 the backlog had been cleared.

104

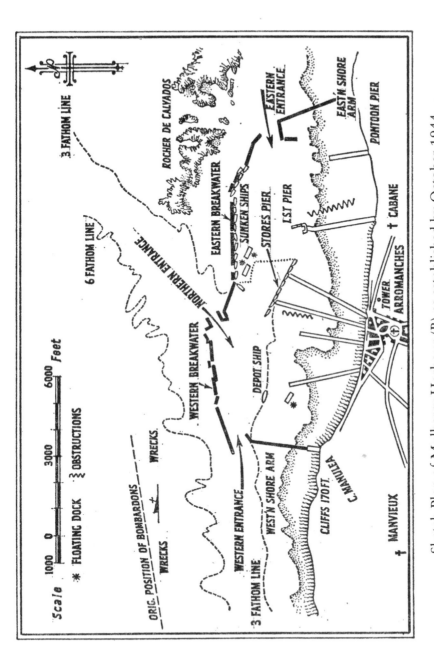

Sketch Plan of Mulberry Harbour (B) as established by October 1944.
Based on a chart produced by the Hydrographer of the Navy.

In the British assault area on D + 1 there were about 100 LSTs waiting to be unloaded, but after 40 had been allowed to dry out on the afternoon's tide, the situation improved and the balance was cleared by the end of D + 2. The unloading of MT ships, however, was being seriously delayed by a shortage of LCTs of which four had been lost on passage, 24 had been damaged by beach obstacles and shell fire, and 16 had broken down, leaving only nineteen serviceable. On D + 1, 24 MT ships and 20 coasters loaded with MT had arrived and a further 25 were due the following day. Fortunately it was found possible to borrow some LCTs from the American area to bring the total up to 85, but even this number was insufficient to compete with a daily arrival of 15 MT ships, so Assault Force Commanders were authorised to retain up to 24 LCTs from the UK-France shuttle service and, with the addition of these, the accumulation of MT ships was reduced to an acceptable figure by D + 8.

Amongst the morning convoys arriving in the British assault area on D + 1 were 60 coasters, but 24 hours later none of them had been completely discharged. This was due in part to the weather and the enemy shelling of *Sword* beach, but also to the Army's insistence on selective unloading similar to that which the US Navy was experiencing. Remarking on this in his report Admiral Ramsay says, "The dangerous practice of 'Selective' loading began at both the British and United States fronts when the situation became critical due to bad weather, causing a shortage of ammunition. It was, however, thereafter continued for weeks with inevitable delays."[5]

It was not only in France that delays occurred in the turn-round of ships during the first few days of the build-up. The congested state of Southampton Water and the Isle of Wight area, where much of the loading was taking place, and the fact that many ships returned there which should have gone to ports to the east and west, all added to the difficulties. There was also considerable traffic in and out of Portsmouth harbour by ships requiring to replenish with ammunition and stores and also oil tankers. Nevertheless, Admiral Ramsay was able to record, "the extensive and complex programme of movements in the Isle of Wight area during the first week of the operation was carried through with only one mistake of any importance."[6] This was a reference to the failure of the SS *Neuralia,* carrying elements of the 7th Armoured

Division, to sail in a convoy on D + 2. The omission was not noticed until D + 5, but the 2nd Army, to which this division belonged, was unaware of its non-arrival.

To return to France, a bonus which helped considerably with the build-up derived from the capture of the small ports in the assault area. Port en Bessin, captured as related by Number 47 RM Commando, proved a greater asset than expected and by D + 8 was averaging 1,000 tons a day. Courseulles, in the *Juno* area, although in a neglected state had not been seriously damaged and was being used on D + 2, after the sandbank silting up the entrance had been moved by earthmoving equipment at Low Water. It too built up to a 1,000 tons a day. Also in the *Juno* area, two 700-feet long pontoons were in place by D + 4 and were accessible two hours on either side of Low Water. It too built up to a capacity of 1,000 tons a day. Also in the *Juno* area, two 700 feet long pontoons were in place by D + 4 and were accessible two hours on either side of Low Water for discharging LCTs. They provided the first means of getting troops ashore dryshod. Unfortunately, due to losses on passage, similar pontoon roadways were not established in the *Gold* area until D + 13.

The continuous presence of the enemy on the left bank of the Orne prevented full use being made of the port of Ouistreham. Also, due to the demolition of the swing bridge over the locks, the excellent quays beyond them, which had survived virtually undamaged, could not be used. Moreover, the Army found it necessary to construct a static bridge in place of the swing bridge to provide an additional line of supply to the 6th Airborne and Special Service Divisions still stoutly holding out to the east of the river.

In the American area, work to bring the ports of Grandcamp and Isigny into use did not begin until D + 7 but by then the establishment of the Mulberry harbours was uppermost in everyone's mind.

THE MULBERRIES

The sites chosen for the establishment of the two Mulberry harbours, off St. Laurent in the *Omaha* area and off Arromanches in the *Gold* area, had been selected so that their construction would not interfere with the assault and follow-up operations of the Armies. In Chapter 4, a short account was given of how the Mulberries originated and were constructed. Rear-Admiral Tennant was in general charge of the operation with Captain A. D. Clarke, USN, responsible for the placing of Mulberry 'A' off *Omaha* and Captain C. H. Petrie, DSO, RN, for Mulberry 'B' off *Gold*, of which he was also the Naval Officer in Charge (NOIC) designate.

The first Mulberry convoys left the United Kingdom on D–day, the handling tugs, control ships and Boom Defence mooring vessels during the forenoon, the Bombardon tows during the afternoon and the Phoenix tows late that night. The moorings for the Bombardons were laid successfully on D + 1 and the first of these floating steel breakwaters was secured in place the following day. The Boom Defence vessels then went on to lay the moorings required for the Gooseberries, Mulberries, depot ships, floating docks, etc., as well as those needed in connection with operation 'Pluto' (the cross channel fuel lines).

As related, the planting of the Gooseberries began on D + 1 and at 0330 on the following day, the first of the Whale (floating roadway) tows sailed from England. These proved so unseaworthy, and such heavy losses were incurred, that whenever possible sections were embarked in Landing Ships Dock and resort was had to towing only when no other means of transport was available and the wind not stronger than force 4.

Although preliminary surveys had been carried out prior to D-day of the areas in which the Mulberries were to be laid, by reconnaissance parties on clandestine missions, it was necessary to check this information. By D + 3 this had been done off Arromanches and the work of sinking the Phoenix caissons began. Off St. Laurent sniper fire and underwater obstacles hindered the work but by D + 10 both harbours were taking shape. In Mulberry A the centre Whale pier had been completed and the special pierhead connected. This enabled the harbour to be brought into use at 1630 that day and the rate of vehicle discharge immediately soared to 78 in 38 minutes, while the time for discharging an LST fell to just over one hour compared with ten to twelve hours using the drying-out method.

In Mulberry 'B', two roadways complete with pierheads were now in use and the rate of discharge of stores had increased from 600 tons a day on D + 6 to 1,500 tons a day on D + 10. The remaining piers in both harbours were making good progress though the losses of material on passage had been greater than expected. Two Phoenixes and five Whale tows, together with two tugs, had been lost. The Mulberries were provided with strong anti-aircraft defences and sixty trawlers fitted with smoke-making apparatus, organised in groups of fifteen, one of which was always available in each harbour, gave added protection against air attack.

The establishment of the Mulberries and Whale roadways took place just in time to solve another problem, the wearing out of the beaches due to the heavy traffic to which they had been subjected. In the *Juno* area Commodore Oliver had already been obliged to institute a system of resting certain parts of the beach to give them time to recover.

SUMMARY OF THE SITUATION ON D + 9 (JUNE 16)

Despite growing German opposition, the Allied armies had succeeded in extending and consolidating their bridgehead. In the American area the Vth and VIIth Corps joined up on June 10 and Carentan was captured two days later. Vth Corps had also made contact with the British 30th Corps on its left on June 11 and Caumont fell the next day. Except to the north-east of Caen, where the enemy had deployed his available armour, progress had been made all along the British front and Bayeux had been captured on D + 1.

By June 15 the enemy had committed three Panzer, one Paratroop and two Infantry divisions in an attempt to stem the Allied advance, but so successful had been the build-up that on June 16 the Allies launched an offensive.

The naval organisation, once the initial difficulties had been overcome, was functioning smoothly. The shipping backlog had been cleared and the Mulberry harbours were proving their worth. Although enemy shelling was still interfering with unloading in the *Sword* area and occasional losses were occurring from mines, by June 15, half a million men and 77,000 vehicles had been landed in France.

Visit of HM King George V1

On June 16 HM King George VI, attended by Admiral Ramsay, the First Sea Lord, Admiral of the Fleet Sir Andrew B. Cunningham, the Chief of the Air Staff, Marshal of the Royal Air Force Sir Charles Portal, and the Chief of Combined Operations, Major General Laycock, embarked in the cruiser HMS *Arethusa* at Portsmouth and visited the assault area, landing on *Juno* beach where he was met by General Montgomery. He returned to Portsmouth the same evening and Admiral Ramsay records, "His visit gave the greatest satisfaction and encouragement to all British naval personnel on the far shore." To his wife he wrote, "I had long conversations with the King throughout the day; he is easy to talk to and likes doing a lot of it himself. He adores the Navy."[7]

Notes
1 ANCXF Report on Neptune, Vol I.
2 B. H. Liddell Hart, *The Other Side of the Hill.*
3 Friedrich Ruge, *Rommel Face au Débarquement 1944.*
4 ANCXF Report on Neptune, Vol I.
5 Ibid.
6 Ibid.
7 W.S. Chalmers, *Full Cycle.*

Right: Commandos equipped with bicycles embarking for France. /*IWM*

Below: Commandos equipped with bicycles disembarking in France. /*IWM*

Below: Air photograph of Mulberry Harbour B off Arromanches after its completion (October 1944). /*IWM*

Bottom: Mulberry Harbour B showing the Western breakwater and the Northern entrance, the Stores pier, and in the distance the LST pier. /*IWM*

Above: Phoenix caissons at the Eastern entrance of Mulberry B and the Boat camber. /*IWM*

Below: The inshore end of one of the floating roadways off Arromanches. /*IWM*

Above: Captain F. J. Hutchings, DSO, OBE, RN, commanding the Pluto organisation with Commander J. H. Lee, RN, on board HMS *Sancroft* during the laying. /*IWM*

Below: The British Prime Minister, Mr Churchill, with General Montgomery after landing in Normandy on June 10th, 1944. /*IWM*

Top: HM King George VI in conversation with Admiral Sir
Bertram Ramsay and General Montgomery during his visit to
Normandy on June 16th, 1944. /IWM

Above: HM King George VI on the bridge of HMS *Arethusa* on
passage to Normandy on June 16th, 1944. /IWM

Top left: HMS *Somali* a Tribal class destroyer. /IWM

Left: A Floating Galley off Arromanches supplying hot meals to men employed on the beaches. /IWM

Above: HMS *Glasgow* receives a hit from a shore battery while bombarding Cherbourg. /IWM

Left: Rear Admiral Hennecke, Commandant of the Port of Cherbourg. */Courtesy Adm. Ruge*

Bottom left: Vice Admiral Morton L. Deyo, USN, commander of the US Navy's Bombarding Force for the attack on Cherbourg. */By kind permission of Admiral Deyo*

Chapter Seven

The Last Phase

THE GREAT GALE

For three days after the King's visit all continued to go well in the assault area, with vehicles, stores and ammunition for the armies ashore being unloaded in satisfactory quantities (*see Appendix VII*). Then suddenly, without warning, nature again gave proof of her capriciousness and for a short while the outcome of Operation Neptune appeared to hang in the balance.

"During June 18, however, two unexpected things happened," writes Dr. Stagg, "a cold front which had been through Iceland the previous day, advanced quickly south-eastward over the British Isles with large increases of pressure behind it; simultaneously a depression in the Mediterranean Sea spread northward into France and deepened. The upshot was a concentration of isobars over the Channel area which produced a north-east wind of force 6 to 7 throughout the two days June 19–20 and only slightly less strong on June 21and 22."[1]

Ever since the invasion had been launched the weather had failed to be such as might reasonably be expected for that time of the year. The Mulberry tows had been hampered by strong cross winds which had also interfered with discharge over the beaches. Low cloud, too, had prevented the Army getting the close air support on which it was relying. During the night of June 17/18 there was the proverbial calm before the storm but, at 0330/19, the wind suddenly started to increase from the north-east. At 0900 it was blowing force 6 and by 1500, gusts of force 7 were frequent, whilst waves six to eight feet high swept over the anchorage and broke along the beaches in long lines of white surf. During the forenoon of June 19, all unloading on the British beaches ceased and ferry craft sought shelter under the Gooseberries and in the half completed Mulberry harbour off Arromanches. Twelve LCTs destined for *Juno* beach, which arrived during the forenoon, were despatched to the shelter of the Gooseberry off Courseulles, but there was insufficient room for all of them and during the next two days seven drifted ashore, of which six broke their backs. The sailing of all further convoys in the shuttle service from England was suspended.

The gale provided a severe test for the Gooseberries and the Phoenix breakwaters of the Mulberry off Arromanches. Some of the blockships settled and the seas broke over them at High Tide, but all the same they saved a large number of landing craft from shipwreck. Where they had been placed really close to one another or with a slight overlap it was even possible to land under their lee.

In the American area off St. Laurent, "The scene inside the Mulberry was one of unutterable chaos," wrote the Commanding Officer of a British craft, which had sought refuge there. "Literally hundreds of landing craft from LCV (Landing Craft Vehicle) to LST (Landing Ship Tank) were ashore, piled one upon another. The Whales (floating roadways) had vanished. The Bombardons (floating breakwaters) were chasing one another madly around the bay. The Phoenixes had cracked. Even the blockships were breaking up and what little searoom remained was packed with wreckage."[2] The losses in fact, amounted to five LSTs and a number of patrol craft.

The Arromanches Mulberry was fortunate, not only in that it was more advanced than the one off St. Laurent, but it received a certain amount of protection from the off-lying Calvados rocks. Also the water in which the Phoenix caissons had been sunk was not as deep as it was off St. Laurent. These factors enabled it to withstand the pounding which it received. All the same, four Phoenixes of the detached breakwater were destroyed and also one at the western end of the Gooseberry extension. The pierheads received only minor damage and the piers themselves remained intact. Nevertheless, the damage to shipping was severe. One LCT had capsized and sunk; an LST, three coasters, a trawler and a small oiler were damaged by grounding. The cruiser HMS *Diadem* collided with Rhino ferry and the destroyer, HMS *Fury,* which had been mined, was driven ashore. The Bombardons broke adrift and either sank or drifted to leeward, providing an additional hazard to shipping riding out the storm, and for good measure the surging of the sea triggered off a number of 'oyster' mines.

On the strength of the calm which preceded the gale, 22 tons of Whale roadway (a total length of two and a half miles) had been sailed from south coast ports on June 17. It reached the assault area safely only to be sunk during the storm.

When the gale finally subsided on the night of June 22/23 the Task and Assault force commanders found themselves faced with a critical situation just at a time when the build-up appeared to be getting into its stride. Altogether, some 800 craft of all types had been driven ashore and most of them damaged and neaped. There was, therefore, an immediate shortage of ferry craft. Moreover, a survey of the St. Laurent Mulberry showed that it had been so damaged as to be not worth repairing, so it was decided that all available resources should be directed to improving and strengthening the one off Arromanches against the onset of winter gales. The four-day storm had, in fact, done more damage than the enemy had been able to accomplish in two weeks.

An Army estimate suggests that as a result of the halt in unloading imposed by the gale, 20,000 vehicles and 140,000 tons of stores were not delivered as scheduled. Whether these figures are correct or not, the effect is certainly reflected in those for the arrival of merchant ships and landing craft in the Assault area which were as follows: June 19 – 239, June 20 – 47, June 21 – Nil, June 22 – 81, June 23 – 281 (*See Appendix VII*). Most serious however, was the shortage of ammunition which developed. It had been a source of great anxiety ever since the invasion began, now it was critical, so much so that an intended offensive across the river Odon could not take place.

Energetic steps were immediately taken to salve as many as possible of the damaged craft. Repair parties landed from their repair ships, HMS *Adventure* and *Albatross,* and Landing Ships (Emergency Repair) No. 2, and began work on the stranded craft piled high up on the foreshore. They were augmented by 250 artificers drawn from the Home Commands in England, while supplies of all kinds including welding kits and structural materials were sent across to France. The salvage teams which had been assembled against such an emergency found themselves working all round the clock. "Due to the energy and resource of all concerned," wrote Admiral Ramsay, "about 600 stranded craft and a few coasters and other small vessels were temporarily repaired and refloated at the next Spring tide on July 8. A further 100 were refloated a fortnight later."[3]

The damage caused by the gale had repercussions in the United Kingdom, where all available repair facilities were already employed coping with repairs to landing craft damaged during the assault, the number of which was greater than had been expected. The extra burden now falling on the repair yards would have proved too much, had it not been for the Combined Operations Repair Organisation (COREP) which now fully justified itself by making the best possible use of the facilities available at all yards along the east, south and south-west coast ports.

As soon as weather permitted, the momentum of the build-up was restarted and every endeavour was made to replenish the Army's stocks of ammunition, which were now dangerously low. Rommel had taken advantage of the lull in the fighting to rest his troops and restore his defences. Luck was on his side for, at a time when his only reserves were the 22nd Panzer Division, still below strength, he was spared having to face the offensive which the Allies had planned and which would have been carried out but for the ammunition shortage.

Force 'Pluto' had taken shelter in Port en Bessin during the gale and its equipment escaped serious damage, so the work of hauling the Tombola fuel pipe lines ashore recommenced as soon as the weather moderated. The first line was completed on June 25, the second nineteen days later, while two more lines off St. Honorine were brought into use on July 2 and 3 respectively, their total capacity in fine weather being 8,000 tons of fuel a day. At the request of the Americans, three short lines were subsequently hauled ashore at the eastern end of *Omaha* beach.

ENEMY MINELAYING ACTIVITIES

Towards the end of June enemy minelaying activities once again gave cause for concern. At the time it was believed that this was in part

114

due to ripening of mines with delay action fuses, as well as to new lays by aircraft and coastal forces during dark hours. As we have seen, during the first two weeks after the invasion, the severest losses occurred in the American area where some ten warships and 24 other craft had been lost or damaged. However, during the period of June 22/24, the only casualty in the US area was the destroyer USS *Davies,* whilst in the British area twelve warships and seven other vessels became casualties. The former included the destroyer HMS *Swift,* a trawler, and two inshore minesweepers sunk, the latter three MT ships and one LCH sunk. Admiral Vian's flagship HMS *Scylla* was amongst those damaged and he transferred with his staff to HMS *Hilary* at 0030/24. The *Scylla* reached Spithead safely under tow. A rigid enforcement of the dead-slow speed order in the assault area brought about a noticeable drop in the casualties due to 'oyster' mines. The minesweepers too, played their part, and by July 3 nearly 300 mines had been accounted for by them, including spontaneous detonations (*See Appendix X*). Although the enemy persisted with his minelaying offensive, from now on it did not seriously interfere with the progress of the build-up.

Closing of 'Sword' beach

The enemy's continued presence on the east bank of the river Orne, and his ability to employ mobile gun batteries and mortars to keep *Sword* beach under fire, was a considerable irritation to those engaged in unloading supplies there. Moreover, the fire became increasingly accurate despite counter-battery fire by LCC(L)s operating close inshore and the employment of smoke. On June 15 the Canadian corvette HMCS *Albernie* and six LCTs were damaged and from then on the landing of personnel was discontinued. The next day HMS *Locust,* Headquarters ship of Assault Group S1, and some ferry craft were hit and it was decided to cease the drying out of LSTs. After a beached coaster loaded with ammunition was hit on June 23, the use of the beach was limited to stores coasters. Two days later the enemy's fire became even more persistent and it was decided to transfer the remaining MT ships and coasters to anchorages off *Juno* and *Gold* beaches. Ferry craft and depot ships followed and on July 1 the *Sword* beaches were closed and the Naval Officer in Charge withdrawn. Although the enemy guns which obliged this withdrawal were only of small calibre, the incident showed, as Admiral Ramsay pointed out, that an exposed flank is not the ideal site for an unloading beach unless the Army can advance sufficiently to prevent the enemy taking it under fire, or alternatively it can bring artillery to bear and neutralise that of the enemy. Neither of these actions proved possible in this instance.

NAVAL ACTIVITY JUNE 17–JULY 5

The enemy's capacity for reaction had been severely reduced as a result of the bombing attacks on Boulogne and Le Havre and eventually he was obliged to transfer boats from northern areas to replace those lost. Meanwhile Allied coastal force activity was mainly directed to the interception of German convoys off the Channel Islands and preventing the evacuation of ships and men from the now threatened port of Cherbourg. On the night of June 22/23 the 65th MTB Flotilla of the Portsmouth command intercepted a convoy of four gun carriers escorting three coasters from Cherbourg to Alderney and sank one of the former and all three of the latter. Towards the end of the month fog was prevalent in the area and such contacts which occurred generally proved inconclusive. On June 26/27, however, HMCS *Huron* and *Eskimo* sank a minesweeper and a patrol vessel to the south of Jersey.

U-BOAT ACTIVITY

Despite a discouraging start, as recounted in the last chapter, the Germans persisted with U-boat operations, appreciating that these offered the best hope of interfering with the build-up of the Allied forces in Normandy. To this end Admiral Dönitz had ordered the transfer of U-boats from Norway and Germany to the Channel area. The Admiralty suspected that this might happen and on June 17 directed that all available A/S Support Groups were to be employed in the Channel and its approaches. They were distributed so as to give the Commander-in-Chief, Plymouth nine groups and the Commander-in-Chief, Portsmouth, one group backed by destroyers which Admiral Ramsay was instructed to make available.

Indicators of the arrival of the enemy reinforcements were given by increased D/F activity in the Western Approaches and off Ushant on the night of June 23/24. The following forenoon numerous sightings were made by aircraft, as a result of which U-971 was destroyed and 42 prisoners taken. Early on June 25 HMS *Bickerton* sank U-269 and 42 survivors were rescued. The U-boats hit back and HMS *Goodson* had her stern blown off by a torpedo. Then at 2200 that night, HMS *Afflick* and *Balfour* made contact with U-1191 which they ultimately succeeded in sinking.

Thick weather on June 25 and 26 restricted the operations of the air patrols and, in consequence, some U-boats managed to penetrate to the Spout where they torpedoed the corvette HMS *Pink*, escorting a southbound convoy 20 miles north-east of Cap Barfleur. The corvette was successfully towed into Portsmouth. At 2130/28 the troopship SS *Maid of Orleans,* returning to Portsmouth in convoy FXP.18, was torpedoed and sunk 35 miles south of Selsey Bill. The following day U-boats torpedoed four Liberty ships in convoy ECM.17, within five miles of the previous day's sinking, but three of the merchant ships were towed back to Spithead and the fourth was able to continue her voyage. Three hours later the SS *Empire Portia* in northbound convoy FMT.22 was torpedoed but she too was towed in. A/S searches in the poor Asdic conditions prevailing produced negative results. However, that evening U-988 was damaged by a Liberator south-west of Start Point and finished off by HM Ships *Essington, Duckworth, Dunnet* and *Cooke* of the 3rd Escort Group the next morning.

The U-boats had reached the peak of their achievements and, although they continued the struggle during the rest of the campaign, their losses were considerable and their successes comparatively few. Nine more U-boats were sunk in July and 21 in August. Admiral Krancke acknowledged his inability to stem the tide of the build-up. An entry in his diary for June 25, made after he had been shown the figures for troops, supplies and vehicles unloaded during the previous 48 hours, which the German monitoring service had intercepted, reads: 'The amounts represent many times the reserves of men and material moved up to the front by us, and offer a clear picture of the enemy's superiority and of the advantages of seaborne supplies, given sea and air superiority."

THE CAPTURE OF CHERBOURG

The virtual destruction of the Mulberry harbour off St. Laurent gave an impetus to the need to capture the port of Cherbourg, so that the Allied armies would no longer be at the mercy of the treacherous Channel weather.

In the hands of the French, Cherbourg was a well-fortified harbour and the Germans had added to the existing defences. Not forgetting the lesson of Singapore, they specially strengthened them against attack from the rear. The only trouble was that there were not enough troops to man them effectively, one of the consequences of Hitler's standfast order to his troops holding the line across the Cotentin Peninsula. Clerks, cooks, signalmen and sailors were pressed into service, the last only after strong protests from the port admiral, Rear-Admiral Hennecke. The defences included three batteries of 11in (28cm) and some twenty of 6in (15cm) guns, fifteen of which were in casemates, together with a large number of 3.5 and 3in guns.

General Collins, commanding the American VII Corps, which was moving steadily up the Cotentin Peninsula towards Cherbourg, was misled into thinking that naval bombardment of the defences would not be needed, such was the speed at which the German forces began to retreat in the latter stages. When, however, on June 23 the enemy troops reached their well-prepared defence lines on the city perimeter, they dug in and held firm. Collins then requested naval gun support as a matter of urgency, but unfortunately the suggestion that a naval bombarding force might be required had only been put to Admiral Ramsay by General Bradley on June 20 during the height of the gale. The ships suitable and available for such duty had to be assembled, replenished and briefed before they could sail. Collins was, therefore, informed that the earliest his request could be met was daylight on June 25.

The bombarding force constituted as Task Force 129 under Rear-Admiral Morton L. Deyo, USN, comprised the following ships:

GROUP 1
USS *Tuscaloosa* (flagship of Rear-Admiral Deyo)
USS *Nevada*, USS *Quincy*, HMS *Glasgow*, HMS *Enterprise* and a screen of six US destroyers

USS *Texas* (flagship of Rear-Admiral Bryant, USN)
USS *Arkansas*, together with a screen of five US destroyers.

Because the ships would need to operate in unswept water, a minesweeping group was attached to each group. The British 9th Minesweeping Flotilla, of eight fleet sweepers, four dan layers and four motor launches, was allocated to Group 1, together with 159th Flotilla of eight inshore minesweepers. 'A' squadron of eight US minesweepers, a dan layer and four motor launches was allocated to Group 2.

The force assembled at Portland, whence it sailed at 0430/25. A plan had been drawn up providing for long range bombarding by both Groups, to be followed by a close-range bombardment by the two Groups combined as required by the Army. As Admiral Deyo approached the French coast he received a request from General Collins to cancel the long-range bombardments as he feared casualties to his own troops, so the bombarding ships took up their close-range positions before opening fire.

As the minesweepers preceding Group 1 turned parallel to the coast to sweep the close support area north of the harbour, they came under heavy fire, the German gunners having held their fire until certain that their targets were within range. The accompanying destroyers made smoke but the enemy was not deterred and the volume of fire increased, so much so that when only half the scheduled distance had been swept, Admiral Deyo ordered the minesweepers to withdraw to the northward. Fortunately, none of them had been hit, for a minesweeper with her sweep streamed cannot manoeuvre to avoid the fall of shot, and no mines had been discovered which encouraged the belief that the area was clear.

A spirited battle now ensued between the two British cruisers of Group 1 and a battery of 6in guns at Querqueville, just west of the harbour, during which *HMS Glasgow* was hit in the port hangar and soon afterwards in the after super-structure. It was not until 1440, and after 318 rounds of 6in gunfire, that the battery was silenced, and then only temporarily. Air spotting was available both from US Naval Kingfisher aircraft and RAF Spitfires. While the Querqueville battery engaged the attention of the British cruisers, the American ships, manoeuvring independently, answered calls for fire support from the Army ashore, but every now and again they were obliged to direct their fire on enemy batteries, the fire of which was becoming too accurate for comfort.

Group 2 also encountered heavy fire as it turned into the close support area and was unable to join up with Group 1 as intended because it became involved with the 'Hamburg' battery of four 11in guns sited a short distance south of Cap Levi. The guns were manned by sailors and extremely well protected with steel plates and reinforced concrete casemates. In the vicinity there were six 3.5in guns and a dozen or more A/A guns. The big guns had a range of 40,000 yards but were unable to train on a bearing east and south of 035 degrees. Admiral Bryant's plan for neutralising this battery, using the *Nevada's* long-range 14-in guns firing from the blind sector, had to be abandoned when he received orders cancelling the long-range bombardment. In the event the battleship *Texas* took on the Hamburg battery and scored a direct hit, knocking out one of the guns. Destroyers laid a smoke screen to give her protection but at 1316 she received a hit from an 11-in shell on the top of the conning tower, which after telescoping a fire control periscope, exploded on hitting a column supporting the bridge, which was wrecked. The helmsman was killed and eleven men wounded.

In reply to a signal at 1320 from Admiral Deyo, asking whether he wished the bombardment to continue, General Collins asked that it should do so until 1500. When, at that time, the Force withdrew, of the three battleships and four cruisers, all but one had been hit or damaged by fragments from near misses. Captain H. T. Grant, *RCN,* of the *Enterprise,* received a nasty shoulder wound from such a fragment but he remained at his post until his ship reached harbour. Of the eleven destroyers, three had been hit and all the others narrowly missed. Casualties for the whole force amounted to fourteen killed and 38 wounded. On the return of all ships to Portland, except the *Enterprise* which went to Portsmouth, Captain C. P. Clarke, *RN,* of the *Glasgow,* suggested to Admiral Deyo that a conference take place on board his ship to discuss the action. The invitation was gladly accepted and the 'main brace' duly spliced.

In the afternoon of the following day, June 26, the German Fortress Commander, Major General von Schlieben, and Rear-

Admiral Hennecke surrendered the port of Cherbourg. The arsenal, however, continued to hold out until the morning of June 27, and the forts on the outer breakwater until the following day. Pockets of resistance on the tip of the peninsula were not cleared until July 1. General Collins readily acknowledged the value of the naval gun support. In a letter to Admiral Deyo on June 29 he wrote, "The results were excellent and did much to engage the enemy's fire while our troops stormed into Cherbourg from the rear."[4]

Although German demolition of the port and its facilities had been so thorough that it was of no immediate value to the Allies, and the harbour had been heavily mined with all kinds of mines and every conceivable booby trap that the enemy could devise, its swift fall came as a shock to the German High Command.

No time was lost in getting salvage parties and mine disposal teams to work in clearing the port. Many acts of great courage were performed in dealing with the highly dangerous legacy left by the Germans and in raising the numerous sunken ships. As a result of magnificent work by Commodore A. Sullivan, *USNR,* and Commodore T. McKenzie, *RNVR,* Principal Salvage Officer on Admiral Ramsay's Staff, and their team of experts, the first freighters were able to enter the outer harbour on July 16 and discharge into DUKWS.

By the end of the month twelve to fourteen ships were able to discharge simultaneously and soon a daily rate of discharge of 8,500 tons was achieved. In September, when the port was completely cleared, this rate was more than doubled.

As soon as Admiral Ramsay was informed of the possibility of using Cherbourg earlier than had been expected, he was able to dispense with some of the bombarding ships and landing craft for the release of which both the Admiralty and the US Navy Department had been pressing for some time. He had had some experience of a too hasty withdrawal of ships from an area before the operation had been completed, so he resisted the pressure put upon him until he considered the moment opportune.

REVISION OF THE COMMAND STRUCTURE

With the situation restored to normal after the upheaval caused by the gale, the time had come to revise the Command structure. At the beginning of July the British and American Task Force Commanders hauled down their flags and Rear-Admiral J. W. Rivett-Carnac, DSC, became Flag Officer British Assault Area (FOBAA), with his headquarters ashore at Courseulles. Rear-Admiral John Wilkes, USN, was appointed Flag Officer, West and Commander US Naval Bases, France (Comnavbases, France). Rear-Admiral A. G. Talbot and Commodores C. E. Douglas-Pennant and G. N. Oliver were withdrawn.

END OF OPERATION NEPTUNE

The above changes, in effect, marked the end of Operation Neptune. Concluding his report to General Eisenhower, Admiral Ramsay wrote, "I cannot close this letter without expressing my deepest admiration for the manner in which the efforts of the many Commands of all Services and of both our countries, were directed and co-ordinated by yourself as Supreme Commander. I deem it a very great honour to have commanded the Allied Naval Forces in this great operation under your inspiring leadership, which perhaps more than anything else has been responsible for the success achieved."[5]

Notes
1   J. M. Stagg, Forecast for Overlord.
2   Kenneth Edwards, Operation Neptune.
3   ANCXF Report on Neptune, Vol I.
4   Samuel Morison, History of US Naval Operations in World War II, Vol XI.
5   ANCXF Report on Neptune, Vol I.

Epilogue

Admiral Ramsay continued as Naval Commander of the Allied Expeditionary Force, operating from his headquarters at Southwick House, until September 8 when he moved to France. On his departure he handed the author a letter, the text of which is given in Appendix XI, expressing his thanks for the facilities with which he had been provided in *HMS Dryad*.

There was still much fighting to be done on the sea, on land and in the air, before the capitulation of the German forces in May 1945. After the fall of Cherbourg and the subsequent break-out of the American armies at St. Lo, the great port and naval base of Brest was isolated and the Germans began the evacuation of their surface forces and U-boats based there and also at Lorient and St. Nazaire. Meanwhile, they took steps to reinforce their 'E' boat flotillas at Le Havre, Dieppe and Boulogne, bringing the total strength up to twenty. They also began to use small battle units in an attempt to pierce the defences of the Trout Line, but the results achieved were small in comparison with the efforts made. The Germans continued to assault the old French battleship *Courbet*, proudly flying a large tricolour and the cross of Lorraine, with shells, bombs and torpedoes, none of which lessened her efficiency as a block-ship.

On August 15 the postponed invasion of Southern France took place and was met with comparatively slight opposition. The German evacuation of the area followed, except for pockets of resistance at places like the mouth of the Gironde, which held out until the end of the war. The port of Brest was captured on

September 18 after a siege lasting 24 days, the 15in guns of the battleship HMS *Warspite* being used to help reduce the formidable defences. Like Cherbourg it had been thoroughly sabotaged, but by then the Allied armies had advanced so far towards Germany that it had lost much of its importance. The port of Le Havre, bypassed by the rapidly advancing armies, after a pounding by the guns of the *Warspite*, the monitor *Erebus* and the bombers of the RAF, capitulated on September 12. Its capture, together with that of the port of Dieppe, removed the need to continue landing supplies over the beaches, the last one still operating, *Juno,* being closed on September 7. Only a few trawlers were left to look after the once busy anchorages, witnesses to the greatest amphibious operation in history. During the period June 24 to September 12, 1,410,600 tons of stores, 152,000 vehicles and 352,570 men had been landed in the British assault area.

The armies' fuel supplies, which were now being pumped into the Pluto depots at Port en Bessin and Cherbourg, needed to be moved nearer to the scene of the fighting, so new cross-Channel pipelines were laid between Dungeness and Boulogne, the first of which was ready for use on October 26.

Although the port of Antwerp had been entered on September 4, the German hold on the islands in the mouth of the Scheldt, which control the approaches to it, was so strong that much larger forces than had been expected were needed to evict them. A naval force of 181 vessels under Captain A. F. Pugsley, DSO, RN, with three Royal Marine Commandos, 41, 47 and 48, and Army Commando Number 4, in co-operation with the 2nd and 3rd Canadian Divisions, supported by the guns of the battleships *Warspite* and the monitors *Erebus* and *Roberts,* opened the attack on November 1. After two days of very hard fighting under extremely arduous conditions, the enemy forces capitulated. Sweeping of the 80 mile channel leading to Antwerp began at once and, on November 28, the port which leads to the heart of Europe was open to traffic.

It was by a cruel turn of fate that the man who had played the principal role in planning and launching Operation Neptune did not live to witness the culmination of the great enterprise into which he had thrown himself with such enthusiasm and success.

On January 2, 1945 Admiral Ramsay, with four members of his staff, took off from the airfield at Toussus-le-Noble in a Hudson aircraft to attend a conference with Field Marshal Montgomery at Brussels. The aircraft crashed soon after take-off and all the occupants were killed. They were buried with naval honours in the cemetery of St. Germain-en-Laye on the outskirts of Paris, in the land they had fought to liberate.

In a speech at the unveiling on August 7, 1946, of the historic D-day wall map, which is preserved as a memorial of Operation Neptune in HMS *Dryad,* the late Admiral of the Fleet Sir George Creasy, GCB, CBE, DSO, MVO, who had been Admiral Ramsay's Chief of Staff said:

"The rock on which was founded the planning and execution of the Naval side of the Invasion operations, was the keen intelligence, the shrewd judgment, the power of quick decisions and the unruffled personality of our Naval Commander-in-Chief. These were backed by his unique knowledge of Combined Operations and his happy gift for co-operation with our brother sailors of that great service, the United States Navy, and the Navies of our Allies and with the soldiers and airmen of the United Nations."

As a term mate of Creasy's, and with the privilege of a personal friendship extending over half a century, the author would like to pay tribute to this outstanding officer who, from the earliest days, showed all those qualities of leadership and exceptional ability which took him to the top of his profession. He bore the heavy burden of drafting the orders for Operation Neptune with unfailing equanimity, and throughout the long weeks of preparation he never spared himself and expected those under him to show the same high sense of devotion to duty.

The scope of the operation was so large, it has not been possible within the compass of this book, to record the countless acts of bravery and heroism performed by so many of those who took part in it. For both sides this was the crucial battle which was to decide the outcome of the war in Europe, and command of the sea and the air were essential ingredients in the Allied success.

Appendices

Appendix One

Details of Special Ships and Craft Employed During Operation Neptune

Short Title	Description	Remarks
BYMS	British Yard Minesweeper	Fitted with Oropesa and LL/SA sweeps for inshore work.
DUKW	A 2½ ton six wheeled amphibious truck carrying 25 troops	Maximum beach load 3½ tons. Speed on water 6.4mph and on land 50mph.
HDML	Harbour Defence Motor Launch	Length 72ft, speed 12 knots, fitted with asdic. Diesel driven.
LBE	Landing Barge (Emergency Repair)	Self-propelled barges specially fitted out to effect repairs to landing craft. Speed 4½ knots.
LBF	Landing Barge, Flak	Former Thames Barges mounting 40mm A/A guns. Complement 5. Controlled by Army.
LBK	Landing Barge (Kitchen)	Converted from LBV(2) and equipped to provide hot meals to crews of ferry craft in the assault area. Cooking capacity 800 men. Oil fired galley.
LBO	Landing Barge, Oiler	Fitted with 33-ton fuel tank for refuelling landing craft, etc. Self-propelled. 4½ knots.

Short Title	Description	Remarks
LBV (1)	Landing Barge, Vehicle Mark I.	A dumb barge fitted with a ramp.
LBV (2)	Landing Barge, Vehicle Mark II.	Self-propelled, speed 4½ knots. Used for unloading heavy stores.
LBW	Landing Barge, Water	An LBV (2) fitted to carry 33 tons of water.
LCA	Landing Craft Assualt	A self-propelled craft carrying 30 fully equipped troops. Speed 6 knots. Carried by LSI.
LCA(HR)	Landing Craft Assault (Hedgerow)	An LCA fitted with mortars throwing twenty-four 60lb bombs for clearing a lane through minefields and barbed wire.
LCA(OC)	Landing Crafting Assault (Obstacle clearance)	An LCA fitted with a horizontal asdic and carrying obstacle clearance units.
LCC	Landing Craft Control	Used by US forces to control the movements of landing craft and fitted with special navigation and communication equipment.
LCE	Landing Craft (Emergency Repair)	Converted LCVP and fitted with emergency repair and fire-fighting equipment. Speed 8½ knots.
LCF	Landing Craft Flak	Converted LCT(3) or (4) fitted with A/A guns to protect assault forces from close range air and 'E' boat attack.
LCG(L)	Landing Craft Gun (Large)	A converted LCT(3) or (4) mounting two 4.7in guns on a false deck over the hold. Provided close support for assault troops during the assault.

Short Title	Description	Remarks
LCM(1)	Landing Craft (Mechanised) Mark I.	Used for ship to shore ferry service of tanks, armoured cars and MT vehicles up to 16 tons/ or 100 men. Speed 5½ knots.
LCM(3)	Landing Craft (Mechanised) Mark III	A large version of the above, capable of carrying a load of 30 tons. Speed 6 knots
LCH	Landing Craft Headquarters	A converted LCI(L) and used as a headquarters ship for the local senior officer in the assault area. Speed 12½ knots.
LCI(L)	Landing Craft Infantry (Large)	Carries 200 fully-equipped troops which are disembarked by two brows in under 5 minutes. Speed 12½ knots.
LCI(S)	Landing Craft Infantry (Small)	Carries 96 fully-equipped troops below decks and 18 bicycles on the upper deck. Fitted with 4 ramps. Speed 11½ knots.
LCP(L)	Landing Craft Personnel (Large)	Carries 22 fully-equipped troops. No ramp. Speed 10 knots.
LCP(L) (Smoke)	Landing Craft Personnel (Large) Smoke layer	An LCP(L) fitted to lay smoke.
LCP(R)	Landing Craft Personnel (Ramped)	Carries 25 men. Similar to LCP(L) but ramped. Speed 8 knots.
LCP(S)	Landing Craft Personnel (Small)	Carries 20 fully-equipped troops. No ramp. Some were modified to serve as ambulance craft. Speed 5½ knots.
LCP(Sy)	Landing Craft Personnel (Surveying)	An LCP(L) fitted out for hydrographic duties.
LCS(L)2	Landing Craft Support (Large) Mark II	Fitted with light artillery to give close support. Speed 11½ knots.

Short Title	Description	Remarks
LCS(M)	Landing Craft Support (Medium)	Fitted to provide close support with machine gun fire and smoke cover. Beachable. Speed 7 knots.
LCS(S)	Landing Craft Support (Small)	Used as control vessels to lead in DD Tanks. Used only by US forces during Neptune.
LCT(3)	Landing Craft Tank Mark III	Carries 55 men and 11 vehicles. Speed 8 knots.
LCT(4)	Landing Craft Tank Mark IV	Same load as LCT(3). Speed 6 knots.
LCT(5) and (6)	Landing Craft Tank Marks V and VI	Similar carrying capacity to LCT(3) and (4). Speed 5½ knots. Length of LCT(5) 112ft 4in. Diesel.
LCT(A)	Landing Craft Tank	Converted LCT(5), armoured. Could carry 2 or 3 tanks with 95mm guns. Used to provide close support during assault.
LCT(CB)	Landing Craft Tank (Concrete Buster)	Carries 2 or 3 tanks armed with 17pdr high velocity guns for attacking concrete.
LCT(HE)	Landing Craft Tank (High Explosive)	As LCT(A) but not armoured.
LCT(R)	Landing Craft Tank (Rocket)	An LCT(3) fitted with 5in rocket projectors to provide HE drenching fire of an area prior to touch down. Length 160ft. Speed 8 knots.
LCV(P)	Landing Craft Vehicle (Personnel)	US type assault craft. Ramped. Capacity 36 men or 3½ tons dead weight. Speed 8½ knots.
LS(D)	Landing Ship (Dock)	A small mobile floating dock capable of carrying a loaded landing craft in a floodable well. Used for making emergency repairs to damaged landing craft.

Short Title	Description	Remarks
LS(E)	Landing Ship (Emergency Repair)	Converted LST(2) equipped to carry out emergency repairs to destroyers and below in the assault area.
LSH US AGC	Landing Ship Headquarters	Ex-merchant ships of about 7,000 tons converted to serve as HQ ships to Force Commanders. Speed 15 knots.
LSI(L)	Landing Ship Infantry (Large)	Merchant ships of 14,000 tons to 8,000 tons converted to carry 1,100 troops and equipped with 24 to 18 LCAs. 16 knots.
LSI(M)	Landing Ship Infantry (Medium)	Small passenger ships of 3,500 to 4,000 tons carrying 400 troops and 8 LCAs. Speed 20 knots.
LSI(S)	Landing Ship Infantry (Small)	Former Belgian cross-Channel steamers of 3,100 to 3,700 tons carrying 240 troops and 8 LCAs. Speed 20 knots.
LSI(H)	Landing Ship Infantry (Hand hoisting)	Former cross-Channel steamers 2,400 to 4,200 tons carrying 360 troops and 6 LCAs. Speed 15 knots.
LS(S)	Landing Ship (Stern chute)	Converted train ferries of 2,500 tons. Capacity 13 minor landing craft launched from chutes at the stern.
LST(1)	Landing Ship Tank Mark I.	*Misoa*, *Bachaquero* and *Tasajera*, ramped ships. Capacity 175 men and 35 vehicles. Speed 8 knots. Beachable.
LST(2)	Landing Ship Tank Mark II.	Capacity 300 troops and 60 tanks. Full load displacement 3,776 tons. Speed 9 knots. Some fitted for evacuation of casualties.

Short Title	Description	Remarks
LVT	Landing Vehicle Tracked or Alligator	A tracked amphibious vehicle, capacity 24 men or 4,500lb cargo. Water speed 5 knots, land 11mph.

Appendix Two

Allocation of Landing Ships and Craft To Eastern and Western Task Forces

	Eastern Task Force	Western Task Force
Landing Ships Headquarters	3	1
Landing Ships Infantry and Attack Transports	36	19
Landing Ships Tank	130[1]	106
Landing Ships Emergency Repairs and Landing Ships Dock	3	3
Landing Craft Assault and Landing Craft Vehicle (Personnel)	408	94[2] 189
Landing Craft Headquarters	11	–
Landing Craft Control	–	15
Landing Craft Infantry	155[3]	93
Landing Craft Tank	487	350[4]
Landing Craft Flak	18	11
Landing Craft Gun	16	9
Landing Craft Support	83	38
Landing Craft Tank (Rocket)	22	14
Landing Craft Smoke and Survey	100	54
Total:	1,472	996
Grand Total:		2,468

[1] of which 37 US; [2] of which 54 US; [3] of which 25 US; [4] of which 230 US.

In addition to the above, 1,656 Landing Craft, Barges, Trawlers, and Rhino ferries were required to assist in the Assault area with the landing personnel, stores and equipment, as well as to assist damaged ships.

Appendix Three

Warships Allocated to the Assault Phase of Operation Neptune

Type	Eastern Naval Task Force	Western Naval Task Force
	(Rear-Admiral Sir P. Vian)	*(Rear-Admiral A. G. Kirk,* USN)
Battleships	2	3 US
Monitors	1	1
Cruisers	13 (1 Polish)	10 (3 US, 2 French)
Gunboats	2 (1 Dutch)	1 (Dutch)
Fleet Destroyers	30 (2 Norwegian)	30 US
Hunt class destroyers	14 (2 Polish, 1 Norwegian, 1 French)	5
Sloops	4	–
Fleet Minesweepers	42	56 (9 US)
Other minesweepers and Danlayers	87	62 (16 US)
Frigates and Destroyer Escorts	19 (2 French)	12 (6 US, 2 French)
Corvettes	17 (2 Greek)	4 (2 French)
Patrol Craft	-	18 US
A/S Trawlers	21	9

Type	Eastern Naval Task Force	Western Naval Task Force
Minelayers	2	–
Coastal Craft	90 (30 US)	113 (81 US)
Seaplane carrier	1	–
Midget Submarines	2	–

In addition to the above, the Home Commands disposed of 20 Fleet Destroyers (of which 4 US and 2 Polish), 6 Hunt class destroyers, 10 Sloops, 32 Frigates and Destroyer Escorts, 50 Corvettes (of which 3 Norwegian and 1 French), 30 A/S Trawlers, 2 Minelayers, 292 Coastal craft (of which 8 French, 13 Dutch and 3 Norwegian), and 58 A/S Groups.

Admiral Ramsay also had 1 battleship and 40 minesweepers in reserve. *The Grand Total of warships amounted to 1,213.*

Appendix Four

Bombarding Ships and Support Craft

Name	Armament	Weight of shell in lb	Maximum Range – Yards	Rate of Fire rpm	Outfit of Shell per gun
Battleships					
Rodney	9–16in	2461	38,400	1.5	116
	12–6in	112	25,100	4.6	150
Warspite	8–15in*	1938	32,200	1.5	110
	8–6in	112	13,600	4.6	150
Ramillies	8–15in†	1938	25,500	1.5	110
	12–6in	112	13,600	4.6	130
Nevada	10–14in	1275	35,000	–	90
	16–5in/38	54	18,200	17	500
Texas	10–14in	1275	35,000	–	140
	6–5in/51	50	34,500	–	230
Arkansas	12–12in	740	24,350	–	–
	6–5in/51	50	34,500	–	230
Monitors					
Roberts	2–15in	1938	30,000	1.5	110
Erebus					
Cruisers					
Frobisher	5	–7 5in	200	23,000	3.0	150
Hawkins	7				
Dragon	6				
Danae	5	–6in	100	19,000	4.6	250
Emerald	7				
Enterprise	6				

* Only two forward turrets in action.
† Only two turrets capable of being manned simultaneously.

Name	Armament	Weight of shell in lb	Maximum Range – Yards	Rate of Fire rpm	Outfit of Shell per gun
Mauritius	12 ⎫				
Belfast	12 ⎪				
Glasgow	12 ⎬ –6in	112	24,800	4.6	200
Ajax	8 ⎪				
Orion	8 ⎪				
Arethusa	6 ⎭				
Scylla	8–4.5in				
Sirius	10 ⎫				
Diadem	8 ⎪				
Bellona	8 ⎬ –5.25in	85	23,400	4.8	360
Black Prince	8 ⎪				
Argonaut	10 ⎭				
Augusta ⎫ ⎧	9–8in	260	38,000	3–10	–
Tuscaloosa ⎭ ⎩	8–5in 25A/A	–	14,420	–	–
Quincy	9–8in	260	18,200	3–10	500
8–5in/38	54				
Montcalm ⎫	9–6in				
Georges Leygues ⎭					
Destroyers					
Tribal class	8–4.7in	50	17,000	5–7	250
Fleet class	4–4.7in	50	17,000	5–7	250
Hunt class –					
Type 1	4–4in	36	19,000	5–10	250
Type 2	6–4in				
Gleaves and Benson					
classes (US)	4–5in/38	54	18,200	17	500
Gunboats					
Flores ⎫					
Soemba ⎭	3–5.9in	120	18,000	–	–
Support Craft					
LCG(L)	2–4.7in	50	15,000	4	140 SAP
					100 HE
LCT(R)	800 to 1,000	29	3,500	–	2 outfits
	5in rockets				
LCS(L)	1–2pdr	2	1,500	10–12	1,800
Mark 1	2–0.5in	–	2,000	700	2,400
	1–4in mortar	10	500	6	120*
	2–Oerlikons	–	2,000	470	2,400

* 60 HE and 60 Smoke.

Name	Armament	Weight of shell in lb	Maximum Range – Yards	Rate of Fire rpm	Outfit of Shell per gun
LCS(L) Mark II	1–6pdr	6	2,000	10–12	200 HE 200AP
	2–0.5in	–	2,000	700	2,400
	1–4in mortar	10	500	6	120*
	2–Oerlikons	–	2,000	470	2,400
LCS(M)	2–0.5in	–	2,000	700	2,400
	1–4in mortar	10	500	6	120*
LCF	8–2pdr	2	2,000	240	1,800
	4–Oerlikons	–	2,000	470	2,400
or	4–2pdr				
	8–Oerlikons				
LCA(HR)	24–60lb bombs	60	380	–	2 outfits

* 60 HE and 60 Smoke.

Appendix Five

Preliminary Bombardment Plan

Target	Locations	Firing Ship	Remarks
Eastern Task Force			
4–6in guns	Longues	HMS *Ajax*	
4–4in guns	Vaux sur Aure	HMS *Argonaut*	
4–4in guns	Arromanches	HMS *Emerald*	
2–3in guns	Arromanches	HMS Neths *Flores*	
Beach Defences	Le Hamel	3 Fleet Destroyers	
Beach Defences	*Gold* Assault Beaches	2 Fleet and 4 Hunt class Destroyers	To close the beaches in immediate support of the LCTs
4–5.9in guns	Ver sur Mer	HMS *Belfast*	
4–4.1in guns	Mont Fleury	HMS *Orion*	
Beach Defences	W. of La Rivière	4 Fleet Destroyers	
Beach Defences	W. of Courseulles	2 Destroyers	
4–4.1in guns	Beny sur Mer	HMS *Diadem*	
Beach Defences	*Juno* Assault Beaches	2 Hunt class Destroyers	To close the beaches in immediate support of the LCTs
Beach Defences	St. Aubin sur Mer	2 Fleet Destroyers	
Beach Defences	Langrune sur Mer	2 Fleet Destroyers	
Beach Defences	Petit Enfer	1 Fleet and 1 Hunt class Destroyer	

Target	Locations	Firing Ship	Remarks
Beach Defences	Lion sur Mer	3 Destroyers	
4–4.1in guns	Colleville sur Orne	ORP *Dragon*	
Beach Defences	E. of Le Brech	1 Destroyer	
Beach Defences	Ouistreham	2 Destroyers	
Beach Defences	*Sword* Assault Beaches	2 Destroyers	
4–6in guns	Ouistreham	HMS *Danae*	
6–6in guns	Ouistreham	HMS *Frobisher*	
Beach Defences	Mouth of the River Orne, Franceville, and Cabourg	3 Destroyers	2 of these acted under the orders of the FOBs with the 6th Airborne Division
4–6in guns	Salennelles	HMS *Arethusa*	
4–6in guns	Le Mont	–	Alternative target for HMS *Arethusa*
4–6in guns	Gonneville sur Mer	–	Alternative target for HMS *Roberts*
6–6in guns	Houlgate	HMS *Roberts*	
6–6in guns	Benerville	HMS *Ramillies*	
6–6in guns	Villerville	HMS *Warspite*	
3–6in guns	Le Havre	–	Alternative target for HMS *Ramillies*
3–15in guns	Le Havre Grand Clos	–	Alternative target for HMS *Warspite*
Western Task Force			
4–6.7in guns	C. Barfleur	HMS *Erebus*	
4–6.1in guns	La Pernelle	–	Alternative target for HMS *Erebus*
6–6.1in guns	Morsalines	HMS *Black Prince*	
4–4.1in guns	Ozeville	USS *Tuscaloosa*	
4–4.1in guns	Fontenay	USS *Quincy*	
6–6.1in guns	Azeville	USS *Nevada*	

Target	Locations	Firing Ship	Remarks
4–6.1in guns	Varreville	HMS *Hawkins*	
Beach Defences	*Utah* Beaches	HMS *Enterprise*, HMS Neths *Soemba*, 8 Destroyers	
4–6.1in guns	Grandcamp	–	Alternative target for HMS *Hawkins*
6–6.1in guns	Pointe du Hoc	USS *Texas*	
Beach Defences	*Omaha* beaches	HMS *Glasgow*, USS *Arkansas*, FFS *Georges Leygues* and 12 Destroyers	
Beach Defences	Port en Bessin	FFS *Montcalm*	

Note: Some of the batteries listed above had been subjected to bombing prior to D–day.

Appendix Six

Notes on German Naval Battle Units Used Against the Invasion Forces

Biber (Beaver)
A midget submarine with a one–man crew and capable of both surface and submerged travel. Weight 6 tons, length 28½ ft (8 3/4m), endurance on the surface 13 hours at 7 knots, submerged 1½ hours at 6 knots.

Dackel (Dachshund)
A long–range torpedo, length 33ft (10m), speed 9 knots, range 35½ miles (57,000m). Fired from Le Havre it could reach a ship anchored off the Orne River. It was pattern running and first used in August 1944.

Linse (Lentil)
A radio–controlled motorboat. Operation was by a unit of three boats of which one was the control and the other two were equipped with explosive charges. The explosive-carrying boats had a pilot who steered them to within striking distance of their target, and then jumped overboard and was picked up by the control boat which had meanwhile directed his boat during the final run-in to its target. The boats displaced 1½ tons and had an endurance of two hours at a speed of 31 knots. They were used in the assault area from June 1944 onwards.

Appendix Seven

Arrivals of Merchant Ships and Landing Craft in France After the Initial Landing of the Assault Forces 7th to 30th June 1944

Date	Liberty Ships	Coasters	LSTs	LCTs	Personnel Ships	LCI(L)
June 7	17	17	4	51	9	–
8	29	29	6	110	11	31
9	35	37	15	50	10	18
10	29	44	31	81	10	28
11	30	25	39	80	9	16
12	17	68	55	57	11	19
13	19	30	56	73	8	30
14	30	25	53	95	9	29
15	34	44	52	76	8	17
16	25	52	62	48	8	18
17	27	29	42	79	7	17
18	30	26	48	89	11	29
19	39	37	48	75	8	32
20	20	22	3	–	2	–
21			The Great Gale			
22	–	30	38	–	13	–
23	–	33	60	165	9	14

Date	Liberty Ships	Coasters	LSTs	LCTs	Personnel Ships	LCI(L)
24	14	39	37	22	3	5
25	23	50	29	39	7	15
26	26	38	55	72	3	13
27	28	27	38	59	7	9
28	35	33	48	–	8	–
29	33	29	41	–	4	16
30	30	24	45	121	5	17
Total	570	788	905	1442	180	372

Note: Not included in the table are Tankers, Hospital Carriers, and Salvage ships with their auxiliaries.

Appendix Eight

Table Showing Rate of Build-Up Achieved Between June 11 and July 4

Date		Personnel Landed	Vehicles Landed	Stores Landed/Tons
By June 11		367,142	50,228	59,961
	12	395,798	56,659	79,485
	13	427,214	62,238	104,975
	14	477,047	68,923	126,724
	15	525,205	77,073	150,924
	16	553,494	83,357	175,496
	17	587,673	89,828	196,464
	18	621,986	95,750	217,624
The Great Gale				
	30	861,838	157,633	501,834
July	1	880,849	163,343	529,398
	2	905,072	171,339	564,644
	3	929,090	117,885	604,328
	4	958,536	183,540	649,568

Appendix Nine

Summary of Warships, Merchant Vessels, and Landing Craft Lost or Damaged Between D–Day and D + 30

Type	Damaged			Total loss			
	Weather	Marine Hazard	Enemy Action	Weather	Marine Hazard	Enemy Action	Total
Warships	12	26	46	–	1	25	110
Merchant Vessels	26	10	16	2	4	18	76
LST	9	5	8	–	–	4	26
LCT	174	1	65	38	1	28	307
LCA	3	1	6	32	–	14	56
LCI	21	–	10	9	–	14	54
LCM	12	–	14	1	–	2	29
LCV(P) and LCP(L)	15	1	3	1	–	–	20
Miscellaneous LC	4	–	–	1	–	1	6
LBV	48	–	–	8	–	–	56
LBO	20	–	–	9	–	–	29
LBW	4	–	–	–	–	–	4
LBE	16	–	–	5	–	–	21
Miscellaneous LB	2	–	1	–	–	–	3
Phoenix	2	–	–	3	–	2	7
Rhino	17	–	–	1	–	–	18
Pontoons	21	–	–	12	–	–	33
Miscellaneous Tows	31	–	–	31	–	–	62
Totals	437	44	169	153	6	108	917

Note: A number of craft damaged but which continued to operate or which returned to England under their own power, are not included in the above table.

Appendix Ten

Mines Destroyed and
Casualties from Mines

| | Mines | | | | Casualties | | | |
| | | Ground | | | HM Ships | | Others | |
Date	Moored	M	A	U	Sunk	Damaged	Sunk	Damaged
June 6	52	–	1	–	–	1	–	–
7	26	–	–	–	–	–	–	2
8	4	–	–	–	–	–	–	–
9	6	7	1	–	–	–	–	–
10	9	1	1	–	–	–	1	–
11	–	–	2	2	1	–	–	–
12	1	–	2	2	–	–	–	–
13	–	7	–	1	–	2	–	1
14	1	–	6	3	–	1	–	–
15	–	–	–	3	–	1	–	–
16	–	–	–	3	–	–	1	–
17	–	–	1	5	–	–	–	–
18	–	1	–	3	–	1	–	–
19	–	–	–	9	–	–	–	–
20	–	–	–	5	–	–	–	–
21	–	–	2	7	–	1	–	–
22	–	–	1	18	–	2	–	–

		Mines			Casualties			
			Ground		HM Ships		Others	
Date	Moored	M	A	U	Sunk	Damaged	Sunk	Damaged
23	–	5	1	10	–	3	–	–
24	–	–	5	6	3	2	2	–
25	–	1	–	3	1	2	–	–
26	–	–	–	7	–	–	–	–
27	–	1	–	10	1	2	–	–
28	–	–	–	33	–	–	1	–
29	–	2	1	–	–	–	–	–
30	–	1	–	13	–	–	–	–
Totals	99	26	24	143	6	18	5	3
				GRAND TOTAL 292				

Note: M = magnetic; A = acoustic; U = unknown.
The table does not include numerous detonations occurring during the night and the great gale.

149

Appendix Eleven

Copy of a Letter from Admiral Sir Bertram Ramsay to the Author

The original is preserved in HMS *Dryad* with other
Mementoes of Operation Neptune

Allied Naval Commander–in–Chief
Expeditionary Force
c/o Admiralty
London S.W.1
7th September 1944

Captain B. B. Schofield, CBE, *Royal Navy*
HMS *Dryad*

On transferring my headquarters to France I want to thank you and your officers and ship's company for the manifold kindness and unfailing help which I and my whole staff have received during our four and a half months in *Dryad*. You turned out of your comfortable quarters to make room for us and you have been given a tremendous amount of extra work in providing for our needs. The readiness and cheerfulness with which it has been done has earned our deep gratitude and admiration. All this enabled us to concentrate unhindered on the final planning and execution of the assault on the coast of France and *Dryad's* contribution to the success of the operation has been a very real one of which you may all be proud.

Goodbye and good luck to you all.

(Signed)
B. H. RAMSAY
Admiral

Acknowledgements

The author wishes to thank all those who, in one way or another, have assisted him with the writing of this book. In particular he would like to acknowledge the help received from Admiral of the Fleet the Earl of Mountbatten of Burma, KG, PC, GCB, OM, GCSI, GCIE, GCVO, DSO, DL, the Lord Zuckerman, OM, KCB, FRS, MA, Vice–Admiral Friedrich Ruge of the Federal German Navy (Retd), Dr. Jurgen Rohwer, Lady Liddell Hart, Rear–Admiral Peter Buckley, CB, DSO, and the Staff of the Admiralty Library, Major–General J. M. Moulton, CB, DSO, OBE, Royal Marines (Retd), Mr. Frank Uhlig Jnr, Senior Editor, the US Naval Institute, Miss S. Glover, Assistant Librarian, Ministry of Defence Library (RUSI) and also my wife whose help, as always, has been invaluable.

The author and publishers wish to thank all those who gave permission for quotations to be made in this volume from the books of which they hold the copyright, viz. Dr. Hans Speidel, Dr. J. M. Stagg, CB, OBE, The Editor *The Mariners Mirror,* Hodder and Stoughton Ltd., Les Presses de la Cité, Barrie and Jenkins, George Harrap & Co. Ltd., Yale University Press, Collins Ltd., A. P. Watt & Sons, A. D. Peters & Co. Ltd., Cassell & Co., HM Stationery Office, Koehlers Verlagsgesellschaft, Weidenfeld (Publishers) Ltd., Hutchinson Publishing Group, Christy and Moore Ltd., Houghton Mifflin & Co., Transworld Publishers Ltd., David Higham Associates.

Bibliography

Blond, Georges. *Le Débarquement 6 Juin*. Paris Anthème Fayard, 1951.

Brassey's Naval Annual 1948. 'The Führer Naval Conferences'. Wm. Clowes.

Carrell, Paul. *Invasion – They're Coming*. Harrap, 1962.

Chalmers, Rear-Admiral W.S. *Full Cycle* (biography of Admiral Sir Bertram Ramsay). Hodder & Stoughton, 1959.

Churchill, Winston S. *The Second World War*, Vols V, VI. Cassell, 1952, 1954.

Dönitz, Grand Admiral Karl. *Memoirs*. Weidenfeld & Nicolson, 1958.

Edwards, Kenneth. *Operation Neptune*. Collins, 1946.

Ehrman, John. *Grand Strategy*, Vol V. August 1943. HMSO.

Eisenhower, General of the Army Dwight D. *Crusade in Europe*. Wm. Heinemann, 1948.

Hodson, J. L. *British Merchantmen at War*. HMSO, 1944.

Holman, Gordon. *Stand By to Beach*. Hodder and Stoughton, 1944.

Liddell Hart, B. H. *The Other Side of the Hill*. Cassell, 1973.

Liddell Hart, B. H. *The Second World War*. Cassell, 1970.

Liddell Hart, Lady. *The Halder Diaries* (privately printed).

Marder, Professor Arthur (ed.). *Years of Power, 1904–1914*, Vol. 2, *Fear God and Dread Nought : The Correspondence of Admiral of the Fleet Lord Fisher of Kilverstone*. Jonathan Cape, 1956.

Maund, Rear-Admiral L. E. H. *Assault from the Sea*. Methuen, 1949.

Montgomery of Alamein, Field Marshal the Viscount. *Normandy to the Baltic*. Hutchinson, 1947.

Morgan, Lt-Gen. Sir Frederick. *Overture to Overlord*. Hodder and Stoughton, 1950.

Morison, Rear-Admiral S. *History of US Naval Operations in World War II*, Vol XI. Oxford University Press, 1957.

Pugsley, W. H. *Saints, Devils and Ordinary Seamen*. Collins, 1945.

Ramsay, Admiral Sir Bertram. 'The Assault Phase of the Normandy Landings'. *London Gazette,* October 28, 1947.

Report of the Allied Naval Commander Expeditionary Force on Operation Neptune. November 1944.

Roskill, S. W. *The War at Sea,* Vol III, Part 2. HMSO, 1961.

Ruge, Vice-Admiral Friedrich. *Rommel Face au Débarquement* (translated by R. Jouan). Presses de la Cité, Paris, 1960.

Ruge, Vice-Admiral Friedrich. *Sea Warfare 1939–1945.* Cassell, 1957.

Ryan, Cornelius. *The Longest Day.* Corgi , 1970.

Schofield, B. B. *British Sea Power.* Batsford, 1967.

Schram, Percy Ernst. *Die Invasion 1944.* Aus dem Kriegstagebuch des Oberkommandos der Wehrmacht. München Dt Taschenbuch Verlag.

Speidel, Lt-Gen. Hans. *We Defended Normandy.* Herbert Jenkins, 1951.

Stagg, J. M. *Forecast for Overlord.* Ian Allan, 1971.

Syrett, David. 'The Methodology of British Amphibious Operations during the Seven Years and American Wars,' *Mariners Mirror,* August, 1972.

Terraine, John. *The Life and Times of Lord Mountbatten.* Hutchinson, 1968.

Tippelskirch, Kurt von. *Die Invasion* 1944. Geschicht des Zweites Weltkriegs, Bonn, 1956.

Warren, C. E. T. and James Benson. *Above Us the Waves.* Harrap, 1953.

Wilmot, Chester. *The Struggle for Europe.* Collins, 1952.

153

Index